DATE DUE

IMPEACHING
THE PRESIDENT

IMPEACHING THE PRESIDENT

ISOBEL V. MORIN

The Millbrook Press
Brookfield, Connecticut

Photographs courtesy of the Library of Congress: pp. 10, 35, 55; Culver Pictures: p. 17; Bettmann: pp. 24, 34, 47, 75, 78, 83, 88, 94, 99, 101, 107, 110, 126, 129, 130; The Richard Nixon Library and Birthplace: p. 65; Nixon Project, National Archives: p. 71; Dennis Brack, Black Star: p. 91; Rotchco Cartoons: pp. 104 (Renault-Sacramento Bee), 113 (Pierotti); Wide World: p.123; The Ronald Reagan Library: p. 136.

Library of Congress Cataloging-in-Publication Data
Morin, Isobel V. 1928–
Impeaching the president / Isobel V. Morin.
p.   cm.
Includes bibliographical references and index.
Summary:Analyzes the Constitution's provision for impeachment
and its relevance to the presidencies of Andrew Jackson,
Andrew Johnson, Richard Nixon, and Ronald Reagan.
ISBN 1-56294-668-4 (lib. bdg.)
1. Impeachments—United States—History—Juvenile works.
2. Presidents—United States—History—Juvenile works. [1. Impeachments—
History. 2. Presidents—History.] I. Title.
KF5075.Z9M67   1996
324.6'3'0973—dc20   95-43820   CIP   AC

Published by The Millbrook Press, Inc.
2 Old New Milford Road, Brookfield, Connecticut 06804

CONTENTS

IMPEACHING
THE PRESIDENT

CENSURE
AND
COMPLAINTS

The crowd that filled the Senate chamber and overflowed into the hallways fell silent as Senator Henry Clay of Kentucky rose to speak. It was the day after Christmas—December 26, 1833. Visitors thronged to the capitol that day to witness the next round in a battle that had gone on since the Twenty-Third Congress had convened early that month. They expected a treat—Clay was one of the best orators in a Congress that included such distinguished speakers as Senator Daniel Webster of Massachusetts and Senator John C. Calhoun of South Carolina.

After unwinding his long, thin frame to its full height, Clay paused to savor the tension that filled the room. Then he got down to business. He proposed that the Senate censure, or officially reprimand, Andrew Jackson, who had been president of the United States since 1829, for exceeding his constitutional authority.

During his three-day tirade against the president, Clay employed all his oratorical techniques. He shouted, then dropped his voice to little more than a whisper. He waved his arms and clenched his fists. He sneered and frowned.

*The powerful orator Henry Clay addressing the Senate.
Clay was very outspoken in his criticism of the actions
of President Andrew Jackson.*

Occasionally he stopped speaking for a moment to heighten the suspense. He began by warning that the president's actions were not only "dangerous to the liberties of the people," but would also soon result in "a concentration of all the powers of government in the hands of one man." Finally, to the accompaniment of repeated applause, he gathered all his oratorical powers for an impassioned conclusion. "The premonitory symptoms of despotism are upon us," he warned. He predicted that if Congress did not act, "the fatal collapse will soon come on, and we shall die— ignobly die—base, mean, and abject slaves; the scorn and contempt of mankind; unpitied, unwept, unmourned."[1]

As Clay sat down, the chamber exploded in a burst of approving shouts. It was one of Henry Clay's best performances.

Clay had been feuding with Jackson for more than a year over the Second Bank of the United States, which had been established by Congress in 1816. In the summer of 1832, Jackson, who opposed the bank, vetoed a bill to extend its charter. Clay, the National Republican Party's 1832 presidential nominee, supported the bank. After Clay lost the election to Jackson by an overwhelming electoral-vote margin, the president ordered his secretary of the treasury, Louis McLane, to withdraw government deposits from the bank. McLane refused. So did his successor, William Duane. Jackson fired both men for their refusals. He then appointed Roger B. Taney as secretary of the treasury. In October 1833, Taney began to withdraw the government funds and deposit them in several state banks. Jackson's opponents sarcastically called these banks "pet banks."

Clay's fight with Jackson had less to do with the bank itself than with the question of the powers the Constitution grants to the president. (Actually, at one time Clay had

BANK OF THE UNITED STATES

In 1791, Congress established, or chartered, the First Bank of the United States. The bank began with $10 million in assets, of which the government provided $2 million. The rest was supplied by private stockholders. (The government later sold its stock to private investors.) The bank was authorized to issue bank notes (promises to pay the holder the value of the note in gold or silver), lend money, and hold money that the government collected in taxes. The bank was controversial. Many believed that Congress lacked the authority to establish it. Congress did not renew the bank's charter, and it stopped operating in 1811.

Congress established the Second Bank of the United States in 1816 after it found that the notes issued by state banks (which could not be redeemed for gold or silver) fluctuated in value. The uncertain value of these notes had an adverse effect on the nation's economy and the government's tax revenue, much of which was collected in the form of notes that were not always worth their stated value. The new national bank, which operated under a twenty-year charter, was also controversial. In 1832, President Andrew Jackson, who did not believe Congress had the authority to establish a national bank, vetoed a law extending the bank's charter. The charter was not subsequently renewed, and the bank went out of existence in 1836.

opposed the bank on the same grounds on which Jackson based his veto: namely, that Congress lacked the authority to establish it.) Clay believed that because Taney had not yet been confirmed by the Senate, he had no authority to remove the goverment deposits. Clay also believed that the Senate's constitutional power to approve or reject presidential appointments to federal offices carried with it the power to rule on the dismissal of such officials. (This question, which had caused controversy since the earliest days of United States history, would later cause serious problems for Andrew Johnson, who was president from 1865 to 1869.)

If Clay had still been in the House of Representatives, where he served for many years, he could have called for stronger action against the president. He could have tried to get the House to impeach the president, an action similar to an indictment in a criminal case. If a majority of the House members voted to impeach Jackson, he would have been tried by the Senate. If two thirds of the senators voted to convict him, he would then have been forced out of office. Clay had been elected to the U.S. Senate in 1831, however. Because the Constitution gives the House the sole power to impeach a federal official, Senator Clay could only call for the president's censure.

Early in March 1834, while the debate on his proposed censure of President Jackson was going on, Clay introduced resolutions to restrict the president's right to dismiss federal officials without the Senate's consent. The Senate failed to act on these resolutions, but voted later that month to censure Jackson for his actions regarding the Bank of the United States. In June 1834 the Senate refused to confirm Taney's appointment as secretary of the treasury. Jackson then appointed Levi Woodbury to this cabinet post.

THE CONSTITUTION ON IMPEACHMENT

Article I, Section 2, clause 5:
The House of Representatives...shall have the sole power of impeachment.

Article I, Section 3, clause 6:
The Senate shall have the sole power to try all impeachments. When sitting for that purpose, they shall be on oath or affirmation. When the President of the United States is tried, the Chief Justice shall preside; And no person shall be convicted without the concurrence of two thirds of the members present.
[Note: Ordinarily the vice president, as president of the Senate, presides over impeachment trials. In the case of the impeachment of a president, however, it was deemed unwise to allow a president's trial to be presided over by the person who would succeed to the presidency in the event of a conviction.]

Article I, Section 3, clause 7:
Judgment in cases of impeachment shall not extend further than to removal from office, and disqualification to hold and enjoy any office of honor, trust or profit under the United States: but the party convicted shall nevertheless be liable and subject to indictment, trial, judgment and punishment according to law.

Article II, Section 2, clause 1:
     The President shall...have power to grant reprieves and pardons for offenses against the United States except in cases of impeachment.

Article II, Section 4:
     The President, Vice President and all civil officers of the United States, shall be removed from office on impeachment for, and conviction of, treason, bribery, or other high crimes and misdemeanors.

Article III, Section 2, clause 3:
     The trial of all crimes, except in cases of impeachment, shall be by jury . . . .

SEPARATION OF POWERS. The fight between Clay and Jackson is an example of the power struggles between the president and Congress that have occurred so frequently in American history. These power struggles occur because of a doctrine called separation of powers. The framers of the Constitution, reluctant to give too much power to the central goverment, had divided its powers among its three branches (executive, legislative, and judicial). The president and Congress often disagree on the extent of their respective powers, however. Such disagreements are more likely to occur when a strong person is president, or when the president and a majority of the members of Congress belong to different political parties and hold different political beliefs.

Jackson, a strong president, had many opponents who feared (as did Clay) that he was becoming a tyrant. Nevertheless, Congress was reluctant to take the drastic step of removing him from office—a step that had never before been taken against an American president. In 1834 the Senate decided to take the less drastic step of censuring Jackson in the hope that this official reprimand would warn the president against further attempts to overstep his authority.

It is doubtful that Congress could have succeeded in removing Jackson from office. Even if the House had impeached him (an action that requires only a majority vote), the Senate would have had considerable trouble getting two thirds of its members to convict him. The Senate's censure vote passed by a majority of 26 to 20—far short of the two thirds needed to convict the president.

HIGH CRIMES AND MISDEMEANORS. Nine years after the censure of President Jackson, the House considered the impeachment of another controversial American president, John Tyler. In 1840, Tyler, a former Democratic senator from Virginia who had voted with Clay to censure Jackson, was elected vice president with the Whig candidate for president, William Henry Harrison. After Harrison's death in April 1841, President Tyler, a Whig who had never really lost his Democratic political beliefs, vetoed almost every important Whig bill. In January 1843 Representative John Minor Botts, a Virginia Whig, introduced a resolution calling for the appointment of a committee to investigate Tyler for various "high crimes and misdemeanors," which Botts believed justified the president's impeachment.

John Tyler (1790-1862), the tenth president of the United States, was investigated for "high crimes and misdemeanors."

Botts listed nine charges against the president, including "a wicked and corrupt abuse of [the] power of appointment and removal by displacing competent and faithful officials" solely for political reasons, the "high misdemeanor" of retaining men in office long after the Senate had rejected their appointment, and "an arbitrary, despotic, and corrupt abuse of the veto power" to gratify his resentment of the Senate's rejection of his nominees for public office. The House defeated the resolution by a vote of 127 to 83.[2]

The Constitution provides for the removal of federal officials from office on impeachment for, and conviction of, treason, bribery, or other high crimes and misdemeanors. (There is a special rule for federal judges, who hold their offices during good behavior.) The Constitution defines treason as levying war against the United States, or adhering to its enemies, giving them aid and comfort (Article III, Section 3). It does not define the other impeachable offenses. The meaning of bribery is clear, but what are "other high crimes and misdemeanors"?

The framers of the Constitution borrowed this phrase from the British parliament, which used it for offenses such as the abuse of power or a betrayal of a public trust. This is not the only interpretation of the phrase in the United States, however. Some Americans believe that when used as grounds to impeach federal officials, the phrase "high crimes and misdemeanors" should refer only to criminal offenses—acts for which a person can be indicted and tried in a criminal court. These supporters believe that to interpret the phrase more loosely would allow Congress to remove a person from office for political reasons unrelated to any misdeeds.

Others believe that an official does not have to violate a law to be guilty of high crimes and misdemeanors.

In their view, an official's abuse of his legitimate authority should also be grounds for impeachment. This view was held by many of the framers of the Constitution.

A provision for the impeachment of federal officials was included in the earliest drafts of the Constitution. Most of the discussion on this subject during the constitutional convention was about what grounds would justify it. An early proposal would have permitted impeachment for "malpractice or neglect of duty." A later proposal called for a more narrow rule—impeachment for "treason or bribery." George Mason of Virginia thought this definition was too narrow. He said that the crime of treason would not include "many great and dangerous offenses...including [a]ttempts to subvert the Constitution." He proposed adding "maladministration" as grounds for impeachment. Another Virginia delegate, James Madison, thought that term was too vague, however. He suggested substituting the phrase "high crimes and misdemeanors against the State." The final version of this provision allowed impeachment for "treason, bribery, or other high crimes and misdemeanors."[3]

The subsequent debates on the ratification, or approval, of the Constitution show that many of its framers thought serious political offenses should be grounds for impeachment. For example, Alexander Hamilton stated that impeachment should apply to "those offenses which proceed from the misconduct of public men, or, in other words, from the abuse or violation of some public trust. They are of a nature which may with peculiar propriety be denominated POLITICAL, as they relate chiefly to injuries done immediately to the society itself." Hamilton's comments appeared in *The Federalist,* a series of publications arguing in favor of New York's ratification of the Constitution.[4]

The framers of the Constitution included the provisions for impeachment because they were worried about the possibility that a federal official, especially the president, might use legitimate authority in ways that were detrimental to the public interest. However, by failing to provide a more precise definition of the grounds for impeachment (admittedly a difficult task), they created a problem that future generations would confront more than once.

When John Botts introduced his resolutions against President Tyler, Congress had little experience with the impeachment of federal officials. At that time, only four federal officials (one U.S. senator, two judges, and one Supreme Court justice) had been impeached. Two of these officials were acquitted by the Senate, one was convicted, and the fourth, Senator William Blount, was never tried because the Senate had already expelled him for misconduct. Because the three trials before the Senate involved judges, who serve only during good behavior, they failed to provide a conclusive answer to the question of whether other federal officials can be removed from office without being found guilty of criminal acts. The question was still unresolved a quarter of a century later when Congress for the first time gave serious consideration to the impeachment of an American president: Andrew Johnson, the only president to be impeached in more than two hundred years of United States history.

2

---⇒●⟨---

PRESIDENT
ANDREW JOHNSON:
REBUILDING
THE UNION

At about ten-thirty on an April evening in 1865, Andrew Johnson got the news that changed his life.

Johnson, who had taken the oath of office as Abraham Lincoln's vice president not much more than a month earlier, had retired for the night when he heard a loud banging on the door of his hotel room on Pennsylvania Avenue. A voice called out, "Governor Johnson, if you are in this room, I must talk to you." Johnson's visitor was Leonard Farwell, a former governor of Wisconsin, who had come to tell the vice president that President Lincoln had been shot at Ford's Theater. A short time later, Johnson and Farwell went to the house near the theater where the president had been taken. After a brief visit to Lincoln's bedside, Johnson returned to his room at the Kirkwood House to await further news. As he waited, he paced the floor, muttering over and over, "They shall suffer for this."[1]

On Saturday morning, April 15, 1865, as a chilly rain fell in Washington, the nation's sixteenth president, Abraham Lincoln, died. Later that morning, a small group of cabinet officials and congressmen gathered at the Kirkwood House as the chief justice of the Supreme Court, Salmon P. Chase, administered the oath of office to Andrew Johnson. In what seemed like a classic rags-to-riches folktale, the former tailor from the mountains of Tennessee had achieved his country's highest office. Johnson was now the seventeenth president of the United States. Only time would tell how well he would fill Abraham Lincoln's shoes.

When Andrew Johnson took office, the South faced a political, economic, and social crisis. The surrender of Confederate General Robert E. Lee to Union General Ulysses S. Grant less than a week earlier had effectively ended the Civil War, but Union armies still occupied Southern territory. The Confederate government had collapsed, and many of the Confederacy's political leaders were fugitives. The war had left much of the region devastated— its crops laid waste, its domestic animals slaughtered, and its cities in ruins. More than a quarter of a million of the South's young men had been killed, and many more had been wounded. Starvation and disease threatened much of the population. Moreover, the South's four million slaves were now free to come and go at will, and while many of them stayed behind, others left their former masters' plantations. This vast throng of homeless, jobless, and often destitute human beings seemed to threaten the entire fabric of white Southern society.

The new president faced two principal problems: how to restore the South to its former place in the Union (a process called Reconstruction) and how to deal with the freed slaves. Congress had already passed the Thirteenth Amendment, which abolished slavery, and a number of states had ratified, or approved, it. (Ratification was completed in December 1865.) Moreover, Congress had established the Freedmen's Bureau to help the former slaves adjust to their new freedom. However, there remained the question of what, if anything, the federal government should do to provide future help. Some believed that additional help was needed, but others believed that such help would lessen the former slaves' freedom by making them dependent on the government.

The success or failure of Andrew Johnson's presidency would depend on how he handled these two situations. This in turn would depend largely on what manner of man Andrew Johnson was.

JOHNSON'S POLITICAL VIEWS. Born in North Carolina in 1808 to impoverished parents, Johnson had no formal education. He became a tailor's apprentice at age fourteen. He later moved to Greenville, in eastern Tennessee, where he established a thriving tailor shop and went into local politics as a Democrat.

An ardent admirer of Andrew Jackson, Johnson believed strongly in the former Democratic president's idea of state rights, that is, a limited national government with the states having the power to handle all matters not specifically designated in the Constitution as federal responsibilities. Johnson portrayed himself during political campaigns (much as Jackson had done) as a man of the people, fighting for their rights against the power of the wealthy aristocrats who dominated Southern politics at the time. He often made venomous personal attacks on these men during his campaign speeches. His fiery oratory made many enemies for him, but it was effective in winning votes. After serving as mayor, state legislator, U.S. congressman, and governor, in 1857 he became a U.S. senator. Despite his success in politics, however, Andrew Johnson remained in many respects an outsider, a loner who seemed unable

Andrew Johnson (1808-1875), the seventeenth president of the United States. Johnson disagreed with Congress on many points including the laws of the Reconstruction Act. He was technically impeached for violating of the Tenure of Office Act, but was not voted out of office.

to shake off a feeling of inferiority because of his impoverished childhood and who rarely consulted others before making political decisions. Johnson's lack of formal education may have made it hard for him to see both sides of complex political issues. At any rate, he was generally unwilling or unable to make the compromises that are so much a part of American politics.

When Johnson entered the Senate, the country was torn by the divisive debate over slavery. A slave owner himself, Johnson saw nothing wrong with slavery. Like many other white Southerners, he justified the institution on the grounds that blacks were inferior to whites. At that time many white Americans in both the North and the South shared Johnson's views. They accepted slavery as either a normal aspect of society or a necessary evil. Even some who wanted slavery abolished shared the widespread beliefs regarding racial inferiority.

Although Johnson agreed with other Southerners about slavery and race, he disagreed on the issue of secession, or withdrawal, from the Union, a subject that was widely discussed. As he saw it, the states had no constitutional right to secede, and those who advocated secession were traitors. Accordingly, when Johnson's home state of Tennessee seceded in 1861, he refused to resign from the Senate. Instead, he remained in the U.S. Congress, the only member from a Confederate state to do so.

When large portions of Tennessee fell into Union hands in 1862, Lincoln appointed Johnson military governor of that state. It was a difficult and dangerous job. Many civilians in Tennessee sided with the Confederacy. Moreover, Confederate armies often menaced the capital city of Nashville. Johnson's stubborn courage in the face of such troubles won him many admirers in the North and may have been instrumental in winning his nomination for the vice presidency in 1864.

Hoping to win support from Northern voters in that year's presidential election, the Republicans changed their party's name to the Union Party. The newly named party, wanting both geographic and political balance on the presidential ticket, nominated the Southern former Democrat, Andrew Johnson, to replace Hannibal Hamlin of Maine as Lincoln's running mate. No one expected fifty-five-year-old Lincoln, a relatively young man, to die in office, leaving his vice president in charge.

Congress was not in session when Johnson took office. The Thirty-Eighth Congress had adjourned, and the Thirty-Ninth Congress was not scheduled to meet until December. (At that time, members of Congress did not take office until December of the year following the year of their election. Thus, the men elected in the fall of 1864 assumed office in December 1865. The Twentieth Amendment later changed these terms.) Of course, upon taking office, Johnson could have called Congress into session early, as Lincoln had done after the attack on Fort Sumter in April 1861, which began the Civil War. Johnson, however, decided to handle things himself for the time being.

JOHNSON'S PROCLAMATIONS. In May 1865, Johnson issued two presidential proclamations. One was a general offer of amnesty (pardon) to Southerners who had supported the Confederacy. Congress had authorized such general amnesties in 1862 as part of a law that permitted the confiscation of Confederates' property. The Confiscation Act of 1862 permitted such seizures as punishment for persons found to be in rebellion against the United States. It also allowed the granting of amnesties to those who were willing to declare their future loyalty. The government seldom used either the confiscation provision of the law (which

THE CONGRESS

Article I, Section 1 of the Constitution establishes Congress as the nation's lawmaking, or legislative, body. Congress consists of two houses—the Senate and the House of Representatives. Since the entire membership of the House is elected every two years, each new congressional election results in a new Congress. Continuity from one Congress to the next is provided by the staggered election of senators, with one third elected every two years.

Article I, Section 4 provides that Congress is to assemble at least once in every year. These annual meetings are called *sessions*. The first session of Congress takes place in odd-numbered years, and the second takes place in even-numbered years. Each Congress is numbered consecutively, beginning with the First Congress, which was elected in 1788 and began its first session in December 1789.

The Constitution originally specified the first Monday in December as the beginning date for each session of Congress unless that body passed a law specifying a different date. The Twentieth Amendment, which became part of the Constitution in 1933, changed this date to January 3. The amendment retained the provision allowing Congress to change the meeting date by passing a law.

required court action) or its amnesty provision during the Civil War.

The other proclamation, as a first step in restoring civil government, appointed a provisional governor for North Carolina and called for a convention of the state's loyal citizens to draw up a new state constitution.

The amnesty proclamation offered pardon and restoration of confiscated property (other than slaves) to those who were willing to swear future loyalty to the Union and to support an end to slavery. Fourteen categories were excluded from the general amnesty, including certain Confederate military and civilian officials and persons who owned property worth more than $20,000 (a substantial sum in those days). Members of the excluded classes could, however, apply to the president for individual pardons.

The proclamation regarding North Carolina—and similar proclamations that Johnson later issued regarding other Southern states—provided that delegates to a state constitutional convention must take the oath of loyalty prescribed by the amnesty proclamation. Johnson later made it clear that he expected the delegates to draft constitutions that recognized the results of their military defeat by nullifying (rescinding) the state secession laws, ratifying the Thirteenth Amendment to abolish slavery, and repudiating the Confederate war debts.

Both the Union and the Confederate governments borrowed money to finance the war. This was generally done by issuing bonds to investors who would be repaid the amount loaned plus interest at some future date. Johnson wanted the new state constitutions to refuse to acknowledge these war debts so that those who had invested in what he considered to be a treasonable enterprise could not profit from the transactions.

Under the president's proclamations, the rules regarding voting rights that were in effect before secession applied to the new constitutional conventions. This meant that blacks, who were barred from voting under the old state constitutions, could take no part in the formal process of restoring their states to full membership in the Union.

CONFLICTING VIEWS. On their face value, these presidential proclamations seemed reasonable enough. Some of their provisions were not significantly different from actions that Lincoln had taken during the war to offer amnesty and provide for civil government in areas controlled by the Union armies. Most Northerners supported the new president's decisions as wise first steps in rebuilding the Union.

The absence of voting rights for black Southerners didn't trouble many white Northerners. Although most of them favored some sort of protection for the rights of both Southern blacks and white Unionists (Southerners who had remained loyal to the Union during the Civil War, often at great risk to themselves), white Northerners generally viewed black suffrage (voting rights) as a radical notion. Many Northern states either denied or severely restricted black suffrage. Lincoln himself, knowing how unpopular black suffrage was, had approached the question cautiously. In his last public speech, on April 11, 1865, Lincoln mentioned the possibility of granting voting rights to very intelligent blacks and to those who had served in the Union army.

At first, President Johnson's amnesty proclamation seemed to be an effective way of preventing Confederate leaders from regaining their former political power. The few pardons granted initially were given only after a thorough investigation of the individual circumstances. Later, the trickle of pardons became a flood. Before long, to the dismay of many Northerners, the pardoned Confederates began turning up in the new state governments.

The new state constitutions drafted during 1865 contained provisions that troubled many Northerners. For example, South Carolina and Mississippi failed to repudiate the Confederate debt, and Mississippi refused to ratify the Thirteenth Amendment. (Mississippi did not ratify this amendment until March 1995.)

The laws the new Southern state governments passed during 1865 regarding black residents caused even greater concern in the North. The so-called Black Codes generally guaranteed the right of the former slaves to marry, to sue and be sued, to make contracts, and to acquire property. The codes barred blacks from voting, however, and severely restricted their ability to own land and to testify in court. Moreover, in an effort to compel the former slaves to work, many Black Codes required blacks to enter into labor contracts each year, with severe penalties imposed on them for contract violations.

The Southern states passed these labor laws because the white lawmakers, who recognized that the South's economic survival depended on its ability to get workers to tend the crops, believed that blacks would work only if forced to do so. Their belief was based at least partly on the reluctance of many blacks to work for their former masters. Such reluctance was understandable, but the white lawmakers interpreted it as a sign of laziness. Actually, the views of the white legislators on this matter were not much different from those of many Union army commanders. The Union officers often imposed restrictions on the former slaves similar to those included in the Black Codes.

The white legislators undoubtedly thought the Black Codes were reasonable accommodations to the blacks' new status as free workers. Many Northerners, however, saw them as oppressive measures that reduced the status of blacks to virtual slavery. Northerners were also angered by reports about the behavior of white Southerners. At first the Southerners, stunned by their defeat, seemed ready to accept any requirements the North might impose on them. Later, however, these submissive attitudes gave way to what many in the North saw as arrogance and defiance. There were also increasing reports of mistreatment of blacks, Southern Unionists, and Northerners. By late 1865 many Northerners had second thoughts about the wisdom of the president's policies regarding the South.

The last straw for many in the North was the large number of former Confederate officials elected to Congress from the South in 1865. When the Thirty-Ninth Congress convened in December of that year, its newly elected members included four Confederate generals, five Confederate colonels, numerous members of the Confederate Congress, and even the Confederate vice president, Alexander H. Stephens. Many Northerners had doubts about the loyalty of the ex-Confederates. These men couldn't truthfully swear that they had never willingly supported the Confederacy (a requirement Congress had imposed on all U.S. officials, including its own members, in 1862). How loyal to the Union were they likely to be in the future?

Andrew Johnson, believing that the South had done everything necessary to resume its proper place in the Union, wanted Congress to allow the new members to take office. The Republican Congress had other ideas, however. Relying on its constitutional right to judge the qualifications of its own members (Article I, Section 5), Congress refused to admit the Southern members.

The refusal of Congress to seat Southern members in December 1865 was based at least partly on practical partisan (political party) politics. Although the Republicans heavily outnumbered the Democrats in both houses, the admission of the Southern members would lessen Republican power. (The Republican Party was virtually nonexistent in the South at that time.) Moreover, the ratification of the Thirteenth Amendment, which was completed in December 1865, would increase the future number of Southern representatives in the House. This was because under Article I, Section 2 of the Constitution, the number of House seats that each state held was based on the entire number of free persons in each state—but only three-fifths of the number of slaves.

The increase in Southern House seats would also increase Southern membership in the electoral college, which voted for the president and vice president. Some Republicans worried about the possibility that a coalition of Southerners and Northern Democrats would elect a Democrat as president in 1868. A few were also concerned that such a coalition might undo the results of the North's victory in the Civil War, perhaps even including the repeal of the Thirteenth Amendment and a reintroduction of slavery in the South.

3

———⟨⟩———

THE BREAK
BETWEEN
THE PRESIDENT
AND CONGRESS

Although the Republicans in Congress wanted to have a hand in shaping Reconstruction policies, they were not in agreement on what needed to be done. A few radicals, mainly former abolitionist crusaders, wanted a complete reform of Southern society. Most congressional Republicans did not favor drastic changes, however. Moreover, they were anxious to avoid a quarrel with the president and looked for ways to modify his policies without antagonizing him.

The Republicans in Congress developed three plans for protecting the rights of blacks and Unionists in the South: a bill extending the life of the Freedmen's Bureau, a civil rights bill, and a proposed constitutional amendment. Before Congress voted on the Freedmen's Bureau and civil rights bills, a few congressional Republicans reviewed their provisions with the president to make sure he had no objections to them. When the president said nothing against the bills, Congress, taking his silence for agreement, passed both bills by overwhelming majorities. To the surprise and shock of the Republicans, Johnson vetoed both bills.

THE FREEDMEN'S BUREAU BILL. Congress had established the Bureau of Refugees, Freedmen, and Abandoned Lands as part of the War Department in March 1865 to help both black and white war refugees. One of its functions was the rental and eventual sale of abandoned and confiscated land to these individuals. The agency, which was to operate until one year after the end of the war, had little real power, however. It also had no money of its own, and was therefore dependent on War Department funds to operate.

In September 1865, President Johnson further weakened the bureau's ability to help the former slaves by ordering the return to pardoned Confederates of all abandoned and confiscated land that had not already been sold. This land included property along the coast of Georgia and South Carolina that General William T. Sherman had set aside for settlement by blacks before the establishment of the Freedmen's Bureau. Many former slaves had established small farms there in the belief that the land belonged to them. Johnson's order forced the bureau to inform the black settlers that they faced eviction unless they agreed to work for the landowners.

The new Freedmen's Bureau bill continued the agency's life for an indefinite period and gave it money of its own. It also gave the Freedmen's Bureau greater authority to help the freed slaves and to punish anyone who violated their rights. Johnson could have based his veto on objections to specific parts of the bill, as Secretary of State William H. Seward recommended, which would have left the door open for Congress to satisfy those objections. Instead, Johnson attacked the entire bill as an unauthorized imposition of requirements on states that had no represen-

As this political cartoon illustrates, Johnson vetoed bills designed to strengthen the Freedmen's Bureau, which had been established in 1865 to help war refugees.

tatives in Congress. Johnson's veto message implied that Congress could pass no Reconstruction laws until it had first seated the newly elected Southerners.

In February 1866, Congress tried to override the veto, but the measure failed by two votes to gain the necessary two-thirds majority in the Senate. Later in the year, Congress passed another Freedmen's Bureau bill over the president's veto.

THE CIVIL RIGHTS BILL. The civil rights bill was designed to overcome the most objectionable features of the Southern Black Codes by giving blacks the same legal rights as whites. It declared that they were United States citizens and guaranteed their right to make contracts, sue, testify in court, own land, and have equal protection under the law. Most members of the president's cabinet recommended that he sign the bill. Nevertheless, Johnson vetoed it as an unconstitutional invasion of state rights. He also said in his veto message that blacks were not qualified for citizenship and claimed that the bill favored blacks over whites. In April 1866, Congress overrode the president's veto—the first time an American Congress took such a step.

By this time even the conservative Republicans in Congress were beginning to turn against the president. They were angered by the hostile tone of the two veto messages and by Johnson's verbal attack on Congress during a Washington's Birthday speech.

Two of Johnson's supporters (Treasury Secretary Hugh McCulloch and Senator James R. Doolittle of Wisconsin), concerned about his tendency to make unwise remarks in public, had urged him not to make the speech that day. Despite his promise to do nothing more than thank the audience for its support, the president told the cheering crowd that the Joint Committee on Reconstruction (the congressional committee that was coordinating all proposed Reconstruction laws) had attempted a consolidation of power that was as objectionable as the Confederate attempt to dissolve the Union. He declared that these men were just as treasonable as the Confederate leaders. Urged on by the crowd, Johnson then named two of the most outspoken Republicans—Senator Charles Sumner of Massachusetts (who was not a member of the committee) and Representative Thaddeus Stevens of Pennsylvania (who was on it) as among those who were trying to destroy the government.

The president's labeling of these two congressional leaders, both staunch supporters of the Union, as traitors embarrassed and angered many Northerners. Some, remembering Johnson's speech at his inauguration as vice president, wondered whether the president had been drunk when he made these accusations. (Before the inauguration, Johnson, who had been ill, took a few drinks to help him get through the ceremony. He evidently misjudged his capacity for liquor, because he gave a rambling, incoherent speech that embarrassed both the government officials and the foreign diplomats who heard it.)

Continued reports of violence against blacks in the South also angered both congressional Republicans and many ordinary citizens in the North. Two such incidents were particularly disturbing. In the spring of 1866 a mob of whites attacked black residents of Memphis, Tennessee, killing a number of blacks and destroying black homes, schools, and churches. In July white police officers attacked an interracial political convention in New Orleans, Louisiana, killing more than three dozen persons and injuring more than a hundred others.

Johnson, meanwhile, had ordered an end to the military trials of Southern civilians, leaving it up to the Southern governments to punish mob violence. On April 2, 1866, he issued a proclamation declaring that the South's rebellion had ended. He then ordered the army to stop trying civilians before military tribunals, basing his action on a U.S. Supreme Court decision.

In *Ex Parte* Milligan, the Court held that military tribunals lacked the authority to try civilians in areas where civil courts were functioning. Despite its sweeping statement, the Court may not have intended to question the legitimacy of military trials in the South. The Milligan decision involved a wartime military trial in Indiana, which had never tried to leave the Union. The situation in Indiana was very different from that in the South, where the loyalty and fairness of local court officials were doubtful.

Recognizing the increasing anger of congressional Republicans over the president's vetoes and his attacks on Congress, several of Johnson's cabinet members advised him to tone down the harshness of his comments. Johnson, convinced that he was right and unaccustomed to making political compromises, refused to change his behavior. His next target was the proposed Fourteenth Amendment, which Congress had passed in June 1866 after extensive debate.

THE FOURTEENTH AMENDMENT. Although it was not clearly specified in the bill, Congress evidently intended to make ratification of the Fourteenth Amendment the price for its admission of representatives from Southern states. The amendment reflected Congress's desire to protect the rights of the freed slaves, prevent the former Confederate leaders from regaining political power, uphold the validity of the Union war debt, and make sure that the Union would not have to pay the bill for the South's rebellion.

The amendment's most significant provision was its first section. This section provided that all persons born in the United States (except for untaxed Indians) were citizens of both the United States and the state in which they lived. The section declared further that no state could abridge the privileges or immunities of American citizens; deprive any person of life, liberty, or property without due process of law; or deny any person within its jurisdiction the equal protection of the law. The amendment also barred former federal officials who had broken their oath of office by supporting the Confederacy from holding future federal offices unless a two-thirds majority of both houses of Congress voted to remove this restriction.

In addition to validating the Union's war debt and repudiating the Confederate debt, the amendment authorized the reduction of the House membership of any state that failed to grant voting rights to all of its adult male residents (a provision that was never implemented).

After he received the amendment, Johnson was forced to send it on to the states for ratification. He expressed his displeasure, however, by sending a special message to Congress questioning congressional authority to amend the Constitution while it deprived eleven states of their constitutional right to representation. He later campaigned against the amendment, urging both Northern and Southern states to refuse to ratify this unauthorized attempt to amend the Constitution while some states were deprived of their right to be represented in Congress. Despite the president's urging, his home state, Tennessee, ratified the amendment in July 1866, and Congress promptly seated its representatives.

Why did Andrew Johnson deliberately antagonize the party that was responsible for his becoming president? For one thing, Johnson, who was still firmly committed to the doctrine of states' rights, was convinced that his plan was the only constitutional method for restoring the South to its previous place in the Union. For another, Johnson hoped to continue in office after the 1868 election. Because a coalition of Southerners and Northern Democrats (both staunch supporters of states' rights) seemed to offer his greatest chance for election, he tried to persuade both groups that he had their best interests in mind.

A NEW PARTY AND NEW PROBLEMS. In the hope of bolstering his chances for a full term as president, Johnson supported the organization of a new political party, the National Union Party, in the summer of 1866.

Although supporters of the proposed new party held a convention, the party never really got off the ground. The convention, which was dominated by Southerners and Northern Democrats, was unable to agree on anything except the need for electing congressional candidates who supported the president's policies, especially his opposition to the proposed Fourteenth Amendment and his demands for the immediate readmission of the Southern representatives to Congress.

Johnson's attempt to form a new political party resulted in the resignations of three of the cabinet members he had inherited from the Lincoln administration. In July 1866, Senator Doolittle asked each cabinet member for a public statement of approval of the forthcoming National Union convention. Secretary of State Seward, Treasury Secretary McCulloch, and Navy Secretary Gideon P. Welles, who generally agreed with the president's policies, gave the requested statements. Postmaster General William Dennison, Secretary of the Interior James Harlan, and Attorney General James Speed resigned after refusing to give the requested approval.

The remaining cabinet member, Secretary of War Edwin M. Stanton, did neither. Despite his disagreement with the president over the proposed Fourteenth Amendment and the National Union movement, Stanton stayed in Johnson's cabinet but secretly cooperated with the president's congressional opponents.

During the summer of 1866, Johnson went on a speaking tour to push for the adoption of his policies. The campaign tour was a disaster. The president repeated the same speech almost word for word at each stop. Before long, hecklers began to interrupt him. Johnson responded with tirades against the so-called Radical Republicans (a term that he and the Democrats applied to all Republicans, even those whose political views were quite conservative). The president accused the Republican Congress of blocking his attempts to achieve reconciliation between the North and South. Many of those who heard Johnson's speeches thought that his speaking style was unsuitable for someone occupying such a high office. A few even wondered, as many had after his Washington's Birthday speech, whether the president had been entirely sober during these speeches.

Johnson hoped that the elections of 1866 would result in a Congress more to his liking. Instead, those elections resulted in a landslide victory for the Republicans, which virtually guaranteed that Republican opposition to his Reconstruction policies would continue in the Fortieth Congress, scheduled to convene in December 1867.

4

CONGRESS
INTERVENES

By the time the Thirty-Ninth Congress assembled for its second session in December 1866, most Republicans believed that major changes were needed in the governments that President Johnson had established in the South. Reports of violence against blacks, white Unionists, and Northerners in the South continued. Johnson's order to end military trials of Southern civilians had restricted the army's ability to punish those who were guilty of such crimes, and the Southern governments generally failed to punish the culprits.

During its second session, the Thirty-Ninth Congress was also concerned about the proposed Fourteenth Amendment's chances for ratification. Three-fourths of the thirty-seven states had to ratify the amendment to make it part of the Constitution. Early in 1867 three border states (Maryland, Delaware, and Kentucky) rejected the amendment. By the end of January 1867, most of the former Confederate states had also refused to ratify it. (Johnson's influence may have prevented Alabama, South Carolina, and Virginia, which appeared ready to ratify it late in 1866, from taking such action.) If the Southern states persisted in their opposition to the amendment, it would not be ratified by enough states to make it part of the Constitution.

A few radicals urged Congress to abolish the state governments in the South and treat the former Confederate states (except for Tennessee) as territories that would be subject to congressional control until they had shown their loyalty and willingness to treat all their residents fairly. Few Republicans were willing to go that far, however. Instead, they passed a law that imposed military rule on the South and required both ratification of the Fourteenth Amendment and black suffrage as the price for readmission into full membership in the Union.

THE RECONSTRUCTION ACT. The Reconstruction Act of 1867 divided the South into five military districts under the command of army officers with the authority to maintain order, enforce federal laws, try offenders in military courts, and remove officials of the Johnson governments, which Congress declared to be provisional only. The act directed the Southern states to draft new constitutions guaranteeing voting rights to blacks. In a reversal of Johnson's earlier Reconstruction policy, blacks could vote for and serve as delegates to the new constitutional conventions, but white former Confederates disqualified from holding office under the proposed Fourteenth Amendment could neither take part in the new state-making process nor hold office in the provisional state governments.

The Republicans had two main reasons for requiring black suffrage in the South. They believed it was needed to enable blacks to protect their rights. They also expected blacks to vote Republican. (Politics and principle both called for the same action.) The new law put white Southerners in a difficult position, however. They now had to decide between giving blacks the vote (a truly radical step for states that had only recently been forced to abolish slavery) or putting up with military rule. Johnson sided with the white Southerners. He vetoed the bill, calling it an attempt to coerce Southerners into adopting measures to which they were opposed and on which they had a right to exercise their own judgment. He condemned the bill as "in palpable conflict with the plainest provisions of the Constitution, and utterly destructive to those great principles of liberty and humanity for which our ancestors on both side of the Atlantic have shed so much blood and expended so much treasure."[1]

Congress wasted no time in overruling the president. It passed the Reconstruction Act over Johnson's veto (an action known as an override) on the same day that it received his veto message. From that time on, Congress overrode all of Johnson's vetoes.

The president had a constitutional duty to see that the nation's laws were faithfully executed. He could, however, use his powers as commander in chief of the army to obstruct the carrying out of the new law's provisions. To prevent this, Congress attached an extra provision, called a rider, to the army appropriation bill requiring that all orders to army commanders go through the army's top official, General Ulysses S. Grant, and barring the president from removing, suspending, or transferring him without the consent of the Senate. Because a veto of the bill would also have cut off all army funds, Johnson signed the bill.

THE TENURE OF OFFICE ACT. Before its final adjournment in March 1867, the Thirty-Ninth Congress took two more significant actions. First, it passed the Tenure of Office Act, which forbade the president from removing any federal official whose appointment required Senate confirmation without that body's consent. The act also declared that any violations of the Tenure of Office Act were "high misdemeanors"—a clear signal to the president that he risked impeachment if he attempted to remove any federal officials without the Senate's agreement.

During 1866 Johnson had dismissed a number of federal officials who refused to promise to support his policies. At that time there were no civil service laws such as we have today, and no large federal workforce. Most appointed federal officials were local postmasters and tariff collectors who got their jobs through political patronage, the awarding of government jobs based on political party membership. Those appointed were generally faithful party members who could be counted on to support the party's candidates in future elections. Johnson's removal of officeholders eventually backfired, however. Concerned about the president's attempt to increase his own political power by removing Republican appointees and replacing them with his own supporters, Congress passed the Tenure of Office Act, with fateful results for Andrew Johnson. Second, remembering how Johnson had taken matters into his own hands in 1865, the Thirty-Ninth Congress called the Fortieth Congress into session immediately following its adjournment.

THE FORTIETH CONGRESS. During its first session the Fortieth Congress corrected a defect in the first military Reconstruction law, which had failed to lay out the procedures for holding new constitutional conventions in the South. Since this law said nothing about when or how these conventions were to be held, the states could simply do nothing and avoid complying with the law. The new law authorized the military commanders to register voters, required both registrars and persons who registered to take strict loyalty oaths, and placed both the conventions and the referenda (referral to the state's voters) on the new constitutions under military supervision.

Shortly after overriding Johnson's veto of the second Reconstruction Act, Congress recessed, but agreed to meet again in July to consider the need for additional Reconstruction legislation. During the congressional recess, Attorney General Henry Stanbery issued two opinions that substantially limited the effects of the military Reconstruction laws. Stanbery said that the military commanders had no authority to remove civil officials from office. (General Philip S. Sheridan had tried to remove from office the Louisiana officials responsible for the 1866 New Orleans riots, an action to which Johnson objected.) The attorney general also said that although the military commanders had authority to keep the peace and punish criminal acts, they had no jurisdiction over crimes committed before the first Reconstruction Act was passed. Moreover, the registrars had no authority to question the statements of persons who registered to vote for delegates to the constitutional conventions. Finally, Stanbery said, the president's duty to see that the laws are faithfully carried out gave him the power to supervise the enforcement of the Reconstruction laws.

After its return to Washington in July, Congress passed a third Reconstruction act, which was designed to overturn the attorney general's opinions. This law gave military commanders the authority to remove civil officials from office. It also gave registrars the authority to refuse to register persons whose loyalty oath appeared to be false, and it required all persons elected or appointed to office in the five military districts to take the oath of past and present loyalty already prescribed for all U.S. officials. A few days

Edwin M. Stanton, who had been secretary of war under Lincoln, remained in Johnson's cabinet, although he opposed many of Johnson's positions. Acting under the Tenure of Office Act, Johnson eventually suspended Stanton and appointed Ulysses S. Grant as interim secretary of war.

later Congress adjourned, but agreed to meet again in November rather than wait until the first Monday in December, the usual meeting date.

Shortly after Congress adjourned, the president took further action to limit the effect of the Reconstruction laws. In August 1867, Johnson suspended Stanton, who had persisted in his cooperation with the Republicans in Congress, and appointed Ulysses S. Grant as interim secretary of war. The president also removed two military commanders in the South who had carried out Congress's Reconstruction laws too vigorously for his liking and replaced them with more conservative commanders. In July he removed General Sheridan from his command in Louisiana and Texas and replaced him with General George H. Thomas, a Democrat from Virginia. A short time later, he replaced General

Daniel E. Sickles in the Carolinas with General E. R. S. Canby.

Johnson's determined opposition to the enforcement of the Reconstruction laws and his encouragement of the efforts of conservative white Southerners to evade these laws troubled many Republicans, who feared that the president's actions would wreck their Reconstruction program. They were particularly concerned about the possibility that conservative whites might manage to defeat the new constitutions that were being drafted in Southern states. If this occurred, and military rule continued, Northern voters might agree with the president that the Republicans were to blame for the continued unrest in the South and might return the Democrats to political power in 1868.

THE REPUBLICAN PARTY TAKES ACTION. The Republicans' fears for their party's future increased as a result of the 1867 state and local elections, in which the Republicans suffered serious losses. Although many local issues were also involved, the losses seemed to be tied to the Republicans' calls for black suffrage in the North. (Congress had already given blacks voting rights in the District of Columbia and the territories, which were under congressional control, and required Nebraska to change its constitution to provide black suffrage as the price for admission as a state.) In 1867, Kansas, Minnesota, and Ohio defeated Republican-sponsored constitutional amendments giving blacks voting rights. The Ohio voters also elected a Democratic state legislature and narrowly missed electing a Democrat as governor.

Most Republicans, recognizing the unpopularity of black suffrage, favored a retreat to more conservative policies. A handful of Radical Republicans were convinced, however, that the solution to their party's problems lay in removing the president from office.

The idea of removing the president from office had been discussed in the North ever since it became evident that the president and the Republican Congress did not see eye to eye on Reconstruction.

The first congressional action came in December 1866, when Representative James M. Ashley of Ohio presented a resolution that was clearly directed against Johnson, although it did not mention him by name. Ashley called for the appointment of a seven-member committee to inquire whether any officers of the U.S. government had committed high crimes and misdemeanors, and whether such acts were designed to overthrow, subvert, or corrupt the government or any of its departments. The House failed to act on this resolution.

Early in January 1867, Ashley introduced a more specific resolution. He asked the House Judiciary Committee to investigate the president's conduct to see whether there were grounds for his impeachment. Another House Republican introduced a similar resolution, and a third member went even further. Representative Benjamin F. Loan of Missouri called for the president's impeachment, declaring that Johnson was "manifestly and notoriously guilty" of high crimes and misdemeanors. The House adopted Ashley's resolution. The Judiciary Committee then began a slow, painstaking examination into every aspect of Andrew Johnson's presidency to determine whether to recommend his impeachment. [2]

The committee made little progress in its impeachment investigation before the Thirty-Ninth Congress adjourned, but the Fortieth Congress agreed to continue the investigation. In July 1867 the committee reported that five of its nine members opposed impeaching the president. Most members of Congress therefore expected the committee's final report to recommend against impeachment. Johnson's attempts to obstruct the enforcement of the Reconstruction laws during the summer and early fall, however, had caused one committee member, Representative John C. Churchill, to change his mind. The report issued in November 1867 recommended, by a vote of 5 to 4, that the president be impeached.

THE ACCUSATIONS. The committee's majority report accused the president of obstructing the carrying out of the Reconstruction laws that Congress had enacted over his veto. The report described Johnson's pardons of Confederate officials, his appointment of former Confederates to offices in the South, his return of confiscated property to Confederates, his repeated vetoes of Reconstruction laws, and his public claim that the Thirty-Ninth Congress was not a legally established body.

Johnson believed that the Thirty-Ninth Congress was not legally established because it had refused to seat the elected representatives from the former Confederate states. He had hinted at this in February 1866 when he vetoed the Freedmen's Bureau bill, stating that Congress should not decide on measures affecting the South while its states were unrepresented in that body. In a speech in August of that year (which Congress used against the president when it finally decided to impeach him in 1868) Johnson referred to Congress as "a body called, or which assumes to be, the Congress of the United States, while, in fact, it is a Congress of only a part of the States."[3]

The majority report recommended impeachment on these grounds. The minority report concluded, however, that there were no legal grounds for the president's impeachment because none of these actions were criminal offenses.

Shortly before the House began its debate on the committee's recommendation, President Johnson issued his annual message to Congress. He referred to the proposed black suffrage mandated under military Reconstruction as "subjugation of the states to negro domination," which he called "worse than the military despotism under which they are now suffering." He questioned the capacity of blacks for self-government, claimed that they had a tendency to relapse into barbarism, and condemned the efforts of Congress to "Africanize the half of our country."[4]

Johnson's message to Congress did nothing to help his chances for avoiding impeachment. The House was still not ready to take such a drastic step, however. On December 7, 1867, the House defeated the impeachment resolution by a vote of 108 to 57. Because a number of House Republicans joined the Democrats in voting against impeachment, the defeat seemed to ensure that unless Johnson supplied the House with new reasons for his removal, he would stay in office for the remainder of his term.

After the failure of the impeachment resolution, Johnson resumed his attack on congressional Reconstruction. Shortly before the end of 1867, he replaced two more commanders in the South, General John Pope and General E. O. C. Ord, with more conservative men, leaving only one of his original appointees in place. General John M. Schofield, head of the Virginia military department, generally agreed with Johnson's Reconstruction policies, although he tried to administer his command in accordance with the Reconstruction laws. Johnson also encouraged white Southerners to refuse to vote on the new state constitutions, which would take effect only after the approval of a majority of the state's registered voters. Johnson's efforts succeeded in Alabama, where a white boycott prevented the approval of that state's new constitution. (Congress later allowed these constitutions to take effect after a majority of those voting approved them.)

Moderate and conservative Republicans were annoyed by the president's actions, but were unwilling to try again to remove him from office. They soon changed their minds, however, after Johnson defied Congress by a deliberate violation of the Tenure of Office Act.

5

===》●《===

PRESIDENT JOHNSON'S IMPEACHMENT AND TRIAL

When President Johnson suspended Secretary of War
Stanton, he acted under a provision of the Tenure of Office
Act. This provision allowed him to suspend a federal official and appoint an interim replacement while Congress
was not in session. After Congress returned, the president
had twenty days to explain why he had suspended the official. If the Senate agreed with the president's decision, the
official would be permanently removed from office. If the
Senate disagreed, however, the official had to be restored
to his former position.

On December 12, 1867, Johnson sent the Senate his
reasons for suspending Stanton. He argued that Stanton
should have resigned when he realized that he could not
support the president's policies. Johnson cited Stanton's
continued efforts to undermine those policies and empha-
sized a president's need to have confidence in his cabinet
members.

The arguments were reasonable, but by that time, the
Senate was not inclined to side with the president. In Janu-

ary 1868 the Senate voted 35 to 6 not to agree to Stanton's removal. Grant then resigned as interim secretary, leaving Stanton in possession of that office.

Johnson, still determined to get rid of Stanton, looked for another replacement. On Friday, February 21, 1868, the president dismissed Stanton and appointed General Lorenzo Thomas as interim secretary of war. Stanton sent word of his dismissal to the House of Representatives and asked for advice on how he should respond. When his Republican supporters in Congress urged him to stay, Stanton refused to leave his office in the War Department headquarters. Meanwhile, both houses of Congress considered the next move.

THE ARTICLES OF IMPEACHMENT. Throughout that weekend, many in Washington feared that a constitutional crisis was at hand. Rumors of an armed conflict between the president and Congress spread. Grant ordered the army garrison in Washington to remain on the alert for trouble and stationed extra troops at the War Department building. The expected clash never occurred, however. The city was still undisturbed on Monday, February 24, 1868, when the House voted along strict party lines (126 to 47) to impeach President Johnson.

The House drafted eleven articles of impeachment (the specific charges against the president). The first eight articles described specific actions by the president that violated the Tenure of Office Act. The ninth article charged the president with trying to persuade an army officer to violate the 1867 Army Appropriation Act. This article referred to a conversation the president had on February 22, 1868, with Major General William H. Emory, the commander of the Washington military district. In that conversation, Johnson told Emory that the provision of the 1867

*The House drafted eleven articles of impeachment against President Johnson—
eight of which described violations of the Tenure of Office Act. John Bingham
and Thaddeus Stevens were among the seven "managers" who presented the
House's case to the Senate. This sketch by Theodore R. Davis ran as the front
cover of the March 14, 1868, issue of* Harper's Weekly.

Army Appropriation Act, which required all orders to military commanders to be issued through General Grant, was unconstitutional. The House Republicans interpreted the president's remark as a suggestion that Emory pass along Johnson's own military commands without referring them to Grant—a clear violation of the law.

The tenth article charged that in numerous public speeches the president deliberately tried to set aside the rightful authority and powers of Congress by subjecting it to disgrace, ridicule, hatred, contempt, and reproach. The eleventh article charged the president with declaring in a public speech that the Thirty-Ninth Congress, as a Congress of only some of the states, had no authority to exercise legislative power. This speech was the August 1866 speech that the House Judiciary Committee referred to in its 1867 recommendation for impeachment. The tenth article also charged that he unlawfully attempted to prevent the execution of the Tenure of Ofice Act, the Army Appropriation Act, and the first Reconstruction Act, all of which were passed by that Congress.

The House appointed seven members to argue the House's case before the Senate. These seven "managers" included two Republicans (John A. Bingham of Ohio and James F. Wilson of Iowa) who had voted against impeachment in 1867 and two of Johnson's most outspoken radical opponents, Thaddeus Stevens of Pennsylvania and Benjamin F. Butler of Massachusetts. The other appointed managers were George S. Boutwell, Thomas Williams, and John A. Logan.

Many Republicans, believing that the president's guilt was obvious, expected a quick trial and conviction. The Senate had already passed a resolution by a margin of 28 to 6 declaring that the president had no authority to remove Stanton and appoint a replacement. In fact, speed was essential. When Johnson was impeached, his term of office had only slightly more than a year to run. A lengthy trial might persuade the Senate that it was better to allow the president to finish his term than to risk the political upheaval that could result from his removal.

THE TRIAL. Those who hoped for a speedy trial were disappointed. The trial did not formally begin until March 30, 1868. It took more than a month for the two sides to present their arguments. The Senate vote did not begin until May 16, 1868, almost three months after the House voted to impeach the president.

Many factors contributed to the delay. The president's defense attorneys persuaded the Senate to postpone the start of the trial until the end of March to allow them a reasonable time to prepare their case. Chief Justice Salmon P. Chase, who presided over the trial, further delayed things by insisting that the proceedings be conducted under the rules for court trials. This helped ensure a fair trial, but it left the door open for endless debate over technical and procedural issues. The defense lawyers and the House managers also delayed matters by indulging in long-winded speeches.

The trial centered on the Tenure of Office Act. There were two main questions concerning this law—whether it was constitutional and whether it protected Stanton.

Today, most historians agree that the Tenure of Office Act was an unconstitutional attempt by Congress to infringe on the president's authority to select his own advisers. The U.S. Supreme Court settled this issue in a 1926 decision regarding the removal of a local postmaster without the Senate's approval. The Court held that an 1876 law limiting the president's power to remove certain postmasters from office without the Senate's approval was unconstitutional. In 1868 this issue was not entirely clear, however. Although many people believed that the law was unconstitutional, others claimed that the Senate's power of confirmation included the right to have a say in the dismissal of officials it had confirmed.

Johnson's defense attorneys, arguing that the law was unconstitutional, pointed to a 1789 law that created the executive departments. During the debate on the 1789 bill, some members of Congress had argued that the removal of department heads (cabinet members) should require the Senate's consent. Others argued that the Constitution gave the power to remove such officials to the president alone. The law as enacted gave the president authority to remove department heads without obtaining the consent of the Senate, but did not clearly indicate whether Congress believed that it could have required such consent. The House managers argued that, in enacting the 1789 law, Congress had simply delegated the removal power to the president.

It was also not clear whether Stanton, a Lincoln appointee, was protected from removal by the Tenure of Office Act. This law was intended primarily to stop President Johnson from removing lower-ranking federal officials from office. Some Republicans wanted the law to apply to cabinet members as well. Others objected because they believed that such a provision was unconstitutional.

The result was a compromise by which the law protected cabinet members for a period up to one month after the expiration of the term of office of the president who appointed them. The compromise language did not, however, clearly state the law's effect on members of a deceased president's cabinet who continued in office under his successor. The president's lawyers argued that because Lincoln's term of office ended with his death, Stanton was protected for only one month after Johnson took office.

The House managers responded that Johnson was merely finishing Lincoln's term of office and thus Stanton would continue to be protected until April 4, 1869, one month after that term ended.

A related issue was whether Johnson's belief that the Tenure of Office Act was unconstitutional relieved him of the duty to see that it was obeyed. Johnson's lawyers argued that his attempt to remove Stanton from office was simply a way of getting the Supreme Court to rule on the law's constitutionality. They pointed out that the president's obligation to preserve, protect, and defend the Constitution required him to resist congressional attempts to limit his constitutional powers. The House managers responded that the president was obliged to obey the law regardless of his belief. Otherwise, the president could decide for himself which laws to enforce and which to ignore.

THE VERDICT. When the Senate met on May 16, 1868, to decide on its verdict, it agreed to vote first on the eleventh article, which seemed to offer the best chance for obtaining a conviction. The vote was 35 to 19 in favor of conviction—one vote shy of the two-thirds majority needed to convict the president. Seven Republican senators (William Pitt Fessenden of Maine, Joseph S. Fowler of Tennessee, James W. Grimes of Iowa, John B. Henderson of Missouri, Edmund G. Ross of Kansas, Lyman Trumbull of Illinois, and Peter G. Van Winkle of West Virginia) joined the Democrats in voting for acquittal.

After voting on the eleventh article, the Senate adjourned until May 26 so its Republican members could attend the party's national convention, which nominated Ulysses S. Grant for president. On its return, the Senate voted on the second and third articles. The result was the same as in the earlier vote—35 to 19. At that point the senators who had voted to convict the president gave up and agreed to end the trial.

Although the trial itself dealt mainly with the question of whether Johnson's actions constituted criminal offenses, there were other factors that affected its outcome.

As is often the case, the relative skills of the lawyers on each side made a difference. Johnson included both Republicans and Democrats on his defense team, which consisted of some of the country's best lawyers. Many of those who attended the trial thought that the president's lawyers did a better job than the House managers.

The attitude of the trial's presiding officer was also important. Chief Justice Chase, who believed that impeachment was unwise, often issued rulings that benefited the president.

The attitude of the Senate toward Johnson's possible successor was another important factor in the outcome of the trial. Since there was no vice president in office, under the rules for presidential succession in effect in 1868, Benjamin F. Wade of Ohio, the Senate president pro tempore (for the time being) would have become president if Johnson had been removed from office. Although the Senate had chosen him over Senator Fessenden in March 1867, the bluff, outspoken Wade was unpopular among his fellow senators. Moreover, Wade's support for high tariffs, prolabor legislation, and so-called soft money (the use of paper money to supplement precious metal coins) alarmed many business and financial leaders as well as conservative Republicans in Congress.

The president's own behavior during the trial also helped him. At the insistence of his lawyers, Johnson stayed away from the Senate chamber and refrained from making inflammatory public speeches while the trial was going on. Moreover, Johnson, who had so often refused to compromise on political questions, arranged deals with moderate and conservative Republicans. In April 1868 he nominated General Schofield as his new secretary of war after being assured that moderate Republicans such as Senator Grimes, who approved the nomination, would vote for his acquittal. In May, after Kansas Senator Ross asked for assurance that the president would cooperate in the readmission of the Southern states under the rules that Congress had imposed, Johnson sent Congress the new constitutions adopted by South Carolina and Arkansas.

As soon as the trial ended, Stanton resigned from office. Four days later the Senate confirmed General Schofield as Stanton's successor. In June 1868, Congress readmitted seven Southern states that had complied with its requirements, leaving only Mississippi, Texas, and Virginia without congressional representation. The readmission bills were passed over the veto of the president, whose promised good behavior did not include refraining from the exercise of his veto power.

Johnson spent the remainder of his term in comparative peace with Congress. He failed to get the presidential nomination he had wanted. The Democrats nominated Horatio Seymour, a former governor of New York, for this office. Johnson was not entirely through with politics, however. In 1874, Tennessee returned him to the U.S. Senate. Johnson died the following year. In 1887, Congress repealed the Tenure of Office Act.

THE REAL ISSUES. Today many historians agree that the claim of Johnson's violation of the Tenure of Office Act was only a pretext for impeaching him.[1] The real issue was political—the president's use of the powers of his office to obstruct the execution of laws that Congress had enacted. Representative George S. Boutwell, one of the House managers, pointed this out during the trial when he said that the president's crime was the subversion of the government. Had the House framed the articles of impeachment in this manner, as Thaddeus Stevens had recommended, the Senate would have had to deal with the clear political issue of a president's use of his legitimate powers to thwart the will of Congress. Instead, the House chose to focus on the narrow legal issue of the president's violation of a particular law—one of doubtful constitutionality and of doubtful applicability to the president's action of removing Stanton.

Perhaps the result would have been the same in either case. Both sides were motivated as much by political considerations as by the legal issues.

The Republicans who voted for conviction were concerned about their own and their party's future, as well as the possibility that Johnson would allow the former Confederate leaders to regain their political power. The Democrats, on the other hand, had nothing to gain by voting to convict a president who shared their political views. The seven Republicans who voted for acquittal were also concerned about the political implications of a conviction. The unpopularity of Senator Wade, the short time remaining in President Johnson's term, Johnson's promise of future good behavior, and concern that a conviction would shake people's faith in their government all played a part in their decision to acquit the president.

The impeachment and trial of Andrew Johnson left unresolved the question of what circumstances justify the removal of an American president from office. The murkiness of this issue was due to several factors. One was the Constitution's failure to spell out the meaning of "high crimes and misdemeanors" as grounds for impeachment. Another was the scarcity of actual cases that could serve as precedents for the future. Furthermore, there was always a question of whether an individual official's misbehavior, whether or not it was criminal, was serious enough to warrant his removal from office.

In the years following Andrew Johnson's impeachment, the United States had to weather many political storms. There were frequent conflicts between Congress and the president. There were also many political scandals, some of which involved criminal acts by high-level federal officials. Despite these problems, however, more than a hundred years passed after the impeachment of Andrew Johnson before Congress again gave serious consideration to the impeachment of an American president—Richard M. Nixon.

Nixon, like Andrew Johnson, faced serious social, economic, and political problems when he took office in 1969. He also had to contend with a Congress that did not share his political views. The situation called for a president who was both knowledgeable about domestic and foreign affairs and skilled in dealing with people. Nixon, unlike Andrew Johnson, had the education and experience to enable him to understand and solve complex political problems. Like his nineteenth-century predecessor, however, Nixon lacked the personal skills that might have enabled him to deal with a hostile Congress and a skeptical American public. Despite his considerable intelligence and analytical ability, Nixon, like Johnson, tended to see his political opponents as personal enemies. Both men's personal failings not only prevented them from solving the problems the country faced when they took office, but ultimately destroyed them politically.

6

PRESIDENT RICHARD NIXON: UNITING AMERICA

Election day, November 5, 1968, must have seemed end-less to Richard M. Nixon, the Republican candidate for president of the United States. Eight years earlier, as vice president, Nixon had lost to the Democratic candidate, Senator John F. Kennedy of Massachusetts, by less than one tenth of one percent of the popular vote. That loss was followed by another defeat that seemed to mark the end of Nixon's political career. In 1962 he had lost the race for the governorship of his home state of California. In a re-markable political comeback, he was now on the verge of achieving his country's highest elective office—or perhaps suffering a third and almost certainly final political defeat.

During the election campaign Nixon tried to main-tain a middle ground on the two dominant issues that di-vided the nation in 1968. The issues were American in-volvement in a seemingly endless war in Vietnam and the violent protests against the war that had plagued American cities and college campuses since the mid-1960s. Nixon

Richard M. Nixon, the thirty-seventh president of the United States, was elected in 1968, a time of social, economic, and political turmoil. Nixon, like Johnson, had to work with a Congress that did not support his views.

promised to get the United States out of the war in Asia and to restore law and order at home. On election night he waited to see whether his strategy had succeeded.

As the election returns came in, Nixon's prospects for victory swung back and forth. He took an early electoral-vote lead, but later in the evening his Democratic opponent, Vice President Hubert H. Humphrey, won in New York and Pennsylvania (with a combined seventy-two electoral votes). Third-party candidate Governor George Wallace of Alabama won in a handful of Southern states.

By early the following morning it was clear that neither Humphrey nor Wallace could win a majority of the electoral votes. At that point there was still a possibility

THE WAR IN VIETNAM

The involvement of the United States in the Vietnam War began while that Southeast Asian country was a French colony called French Indo-China. After the end of World War II, Vietnam tried to establish its independence from France. Although the United States sympathized with Vietnam, it gave financial support to France in its fight to hold onto the colony. It did so because it opposed the Communist leader of the Vietnamese rebels, Ho Chi Minh, and because it wanted to keep France as an ally against attempts at Communist domination of western Europe.

After the Vietnamese defeated the French in 1954, an international agreement temporarily divided Vietnam into two countries pending the holding of a national election. The election, which most observers expected to result in a Communist victory, was not held. Instead, Communist North Vietnam tried to overrun South Vietnam. The United States provided military advisers, equipment, and money to South Vietnam, but the communists gained ground.

After North Vietnamese naval units fired on an American destroyer in the Gulf of Tonkin, Congress passed a resolution on August 7, 1964, authorizing President Lyndon B. Johnson to take all necessary measures to repel armed attack in Vietnam. Following the passage of this resolution, American air and ground forces fought the North Vietnamese until January 1973, when an international agreement ended the war.

In 1975, Vietnam was reunified under Communist control. The United States established diplomatic relations with Vietnam's Communist government in 1995.

that Nixon would not win an electoral-vote majority either, which would send the election into the House of Representatives. The election remained in doubt until later that day, when Nixon won in Illinois, giving him a total of 301 electoral votes—31 more than the 270 he needed to win.

THE NEW PRESIDENT'S CHALLENGES. Shortly after Humphrey conceded the election, Nixon announced to his supporters that his great objective as president would be to bring the American people together. It was a tall order. Nixon had won only slightly more than 43 percent of the popular vote. Moreover, he would have to work with a Democratic Congress. Whether he could achieve his stated goal would depend largely on what manner of man Richard Nixon was.

Born on January 9, 1913, in Yorba Linda, California, Richard Nixon grew up in relative poverty in nearby Whittier. After graduation from Whittier College, Nixon won a scholarship to Duke University School of Law, from which he graduated third in his class. Afterward, he applied to several prominent New York law firms, but despite his impressive academic record and his election as president of the student law association at Duke, Nixon failed to land a job. Instead, he returned to Whittier to practice law.

After a brief stint in a wartime federal agency during World War II, Nixon became a commissioned officer in the U.S. Navy. In 1946, after returning from military service, Nixon entered politics, winning a seat in the U.S. House of Representatives in his first try for public office. In 1950, Nixon defeated Representative Helen Gahagan Douglas in a race for the U.S. Senate. In 1952, at age thirty-nine, he was elected vice president under President Dwight D. Eisenhower, an office he held for eight years.

Nixon's background and personality deeply affected his political career. Despite his early successes and his long experience in public life, Nixon was shy and awkward in dealing with others. Like Andrew Johnson, who was president a century earlier, Nixon never seemed able to shake his perception of himself as the poor boy from the wrong part of town, unable to win acceptance from his better-off neighbors. Nixon, like Johnson, remained a loner throughout his political career, appearing to trust only a small group of close friends. He particularly distrusted federal civil servants, whom he suspected of willfully trying to obstruct his policies, and journalists, whose reporting he thought was biased against him.

Nixon's belief that he was surrounded by enemies had some basis in fact. Many of his political opponents disliked Nixon personally, believing that he had won elections in the past by unfairly implying that his opponents were either communist sympathizers or too naive to recognize the dangers of Communism.

During the 1952 election campaign, Nixon opponents accused him of accumulating a secret fund of donations from wealthy supporters. The revelation of Nixon's suspected political corruption, coming amid Republican denunciations of corruption among Democrats, resulted in calls for Nixon's withdrawal from the vice presidential campaign. Instead, Nixon defended himself in a televised speech that produced a wave of public support for his candidacy. Nixon remained on the Republican ticket, but the incident added to his suspicions that his political enemies were bent on his destruction.

Early in his political career Nixon's opponents, offended by what they regarded as his political dirty tricks, began to call him "Tricky Dicky." The nickname continued to haunt him after the election. As inauguration day drew near, many Americans wondered whether, as *Time* magazine put it, Richard Nixon was "wholly to be trusted."[1]

THE KISSINGER TAPS. After his inauguration, Nixon tried to end American involvement in the Vietnam war, as he had promised during the election campaign. He feared, however, that withdrawing American assistance to South Vietnam too quickly could result in a Communist takeover of that country. A premature withdrawal might also be seen as a sign of weakness that could threaten America's position as a world leader. Nixon therefore increased the military pressure on North Vietnam while his national security adviser, Henry Kissinger, engaged in a series of secret negotiations with the North Vietnamese government—negotiations in which Kissinger bypassed both the state and defense secretaries.

When Nixon learned early in 1969 that Vietnamese Communists were massing stockpiles of weapons in Cambodia (which was officially neutral), he decided to eliminate this threat to South Vietnam's survival. Because he was worried about congressional and public opposition to a violation of Cambodian neutrality, he secretly ordered American planes to bomb the Cambodian sites. In May 1969, *The New York Times* disclosed the bombings, triggering an outburst of protests against the war and against Nixon himself.

Both Nixon and Kissinger were anxious to find out who was responsible for the disclosure. To help with this investigation, Attorney General John Mitchell authorized the Federal Bureau of Investigation (FBI) to install a series of wiretaps on the telephones of federal officials and journalists to enable that agency to listen to their telephone conversations. The reports on the wiretapped conversations were distributed to Nixon and a few of his top aides, but the records of the so-called Kissinger taps were not kept with the FBI's routine wiretap files. Moreover, the Nixon administration failed to ask for a court order for these wiretaps, some of which continued until early in 1971.

This type of wiretapping was controversial. The Nixon administration justified it on grounds of national security, but some people feared that in the absence of adequate safeguards it could be used to control political opposition as well as to thwart attempts to subvert or overthrow the government. The Supreme Court eventually agreed with those who opposed unrestricted government wiretapping. In 1972 the Supreme Court held (in a case not related to the Kissinger taps) that tapping the telephones of domestic individuals or groups without a court order violated the Fourth Amendment's protection against unreasonable searches and seizures.

TROUBLE AT HOME AND THE FBI. Meanwhile, the war in Vietnam continued to cause trouble at home. In 1970, after Nixon ordered American troops into Cambodia to clean out the remaining stockpiles of weapons and supplies, a new wave of protests, many of which were accompanied by violence, swept across the country. Nixon, who suspected that the violence was part of an organized plot to subvert or overthrow the government, appointed an interagency committee of top intelligence officials to consider ways of dealing with the disturbances. J. Edgar Hoover, the FBI director, headed the committee, but most of its work was directed by a White House staff member, Tom Huston.

Huston's comprehensive plan for controlling subversive activities included wiretapping, burglaries, the opening of suspected persons' mail, and the increased use of undercover agents to spy on radical organizations. Nixon

Nixon and chief domestic policy adviser John Ehrlichman and White House chief of staff H. R. Haldeman. Because of his persistent suspicions that he was being undermined, Nixon assigned and hired staff to conduct "special investigations."

initially approved the plan, but withdrew his approval a few days later because Hoover and Mitchell objected to its illegal features, such as unauthorized opening of mail and burglaries. The plan became the model, however, for later undercover activities directed by White House staff members.

THE PENTAGON PAPERS AND THE PLUMBERS. In June 1971 a controversy arose over a series of newspaper articles that included excerpts from a government report on American

NIXON'S WHITE HOUSE STAFF

Henry Kissinger—Nixon's national security adviser until August 1973, when he became secretary of state.

H. R. Haldeman—White House chief of staff until May 1973. These eight men reported to Haldeman:

Gordon C. Strachan—Haldeman's principal political assistant beginning in March 1971.

Alexander P. Butterfield—deputy assistant to the president.

Hugh W. Sloan, Jr.—staff assistant to the president.

John W. Dean—counsel to the president beginning in July 1970.

Jeb Stuart Magruder—special assistant to the president.

Charles W. Colson—special counsel to the president.

Frederick C. LaRue—special consultant to the president.

Tom Huston—an assistant to Haldeman.

John D. Ehrlichman—counsel to the president from January to November 1969, when he became Nixon's chief assistant for domestic policy. These four men reported to Ehrlichman:

Egil Krogh—Ehrlichman's deputy and member of Special Investigations Unit (called the Plumbers).

G. Gordon Liddy—hired by Ehrlichman as member of Special Investigations Unit

E. Howard Hunt—member of Special Investigations Unit; also worked for Charles Colson.

John J. Caulfield—staff assistant to Ehrlichman; also worked for John Dean.

involvement in Vietnam. This material, some of which was classified as "top secret," became known as the Pentagon Papers. Although the published information dealt only with events during previous administrations, Nixon thought that the articles were deliberate attempts to undermine his presidency.

He was also concerned about a report (later discredited) that some of the papers had been given to the Soviet embassy in Washington, D.C. If the material in Soviet hands included information about current government activities, both American foreign policy and American intelligence operations could be harmed. The Nixon administration tried to get the courts to stop the newspapers from publishing any more material from the Pentagon Papers, but the Supreme Court ruled on June 30, 1971, that the government had failed to prove that the publication of these documents endangered national security.

Shortly after the Supreme Court decision, Nixon told his chief domestic policy adviser, John Ehrlichman, to have someone in the White House take responsibility for investigating the Pentagon Papers case and any other leaks of government information that might occur. (By that time Nixon's distrust of government officials extended even to Hoover, the FBI director.)

Ehrlichman appointed his own deputy, Egil Krogh, and one of Kissinger's assistants, David Young, to handle the investigations under his supervision. Two veteran intelligence agents, E. Howard Hunt and G. Gordon Liddy, assisted Krogh and Young. Hunt, a former Central Intelligence Agency (CIA) employee, was already on the White House payroll as a consultant for White House special counsel Charles Colson. (Hunt's "consulting" consisted primarily of undercover political activities under Colson's supervision.) Liddy was a former FBI agent hired by Ehrlichman on Krogh's recommendation. The team was officially called the Special Investigations Unit, but since it was formed to stop leaks, it became known as the Plumbers.

One of the Plumbers' first jobs involved an effort to discredit Daniel Ellsberg, a former member of the staff of the National Security Council (NSC). Ellsberg, who was responsible for the leak of the Pentagon Papers, was then awaiting trial for the theft of these documents. (Colson was also working on the attempt to discredit Ellsberg.) In September 1971, Hunt and Liddy, with the help of the CIA, staged a covert operation to search the files of Dr. Lewis Fielding, a psychiatrist that Ellsberg had consulted, for damaging information on Ellsberg. Ehrlichman had approved the operation, which was actually a burglary of the doctor's office, with the caution that it must not be traceable. It has never been conclusively established what, if anything, Hunt and Liddy found as a result of the burglary.

Former FBI agent G. Gordon Liddy was hired by John Ehrlichman as a member of the Special Investigations Unit, later known as the Plumbers. Liddy later played a central role in the burglary known as the Watergate break-in.

Despite the efforts of the Plumbers, the leaks continued. In December 1971, during an investigation of a leak
of government information regarding the war then being
waged between India and Pakistan, the Plumbers and Defense Department officials discovered a bizarre spying
operation in the National Security Council. A naval petty
officer filched NSC documents and passed them to his superior officer, an admiral assigned to liaison duties between
the Joint Chiefs of Staff and the NSC.

The spying, which had been going on for some time,
was apparently simply the military officials' way of making sure they knew what was going on in the NSC. However, to a jittery president and his staff it looked suspi-
ciously like preparations for a military seizure of power.
The guilty officers were transferred, and the matter was
hushed up, but the incident added to the atmosphere of
distrust and suspicion that had filled the White House since
the early days of the Nixon administration. As 1971 drew
to a close, Nixon's stated goal of bringing Americans together seemed far from being realized. Many wondered
whether Nixon's actions as president had actually further
divided a troubled nation.

THE REELECTION CAMPAIGN
AND WATERGATE

On January 7, 1972, President Nixon formally announced his candidacy for reelection. Faced with only token opposition from within the Republican Party, he seemed to be in a good position to win a second term. Kissinger's secret negotiations had opened the door to the reestablishment of friendly relations with China after almost a quarter of a century of hostility and had improved relations with the Soviet Union. Nixon planned to visit China in February and the Soviet Union in May for discussions with the leaders of the two countries—the first time an American president would visit both of these Communist powers. Because of his accomplishments, *Time* magazine named Nixon its 1971 Man of the Year.

During an interview with *Time* staff reporters and editors in December 1971, Nixon said that he would not engage in any political activities until after the Republican National Convention the following August. The reelection campaign had never been far from Nixon's thoughts, however. Ever since his narrow victory in 1968, Nixon had worried about being a one-term president—something he was determined to avoid at all costs.

THE CAMPAIGN. Nixon began making plans for the 1972 campaign shortly after the 1970 elections. The Committee to Re-Elect the President, formed in the spring of 1971, operated independently of the Republican National Committee, partly to give it the apearance of a nonpartisan organization and partly to keep its activities under White House control. Nixon's opponents sarcastically referred to the reelection committee as CREEP.

    H. R. Haldeman, Nixon's White House chief of staff, played an active part in its formation. Several members of the White House staff joined the committee. One of Haldeman's assistants, Jeb Stuart Magruder, acted as its

Jeb Stuart Magruder, deputy director of President Nixon's reelection campaign from 1971 to 1972, acknowledged he had made a "disastrous decision" when he approved the Watergate break-in.

CREEP, THE COMMITTEE TO RE-ELECT THE PRESIDENT

Jeb Stuart Magruder—director from May 1971 until April 1972, when he became deputy director.

John Mitchell—Nixon's attorney general until April 1972, when he resigned to become the committee's director.

Maurice Stans—Nixon's commerce secretary until February 1972, when he became the committee's finance chairman.

Hugh W. Sloan, Jr.—committee treasurer.

G. Gordon Liddy—counsel to the committee.

James W. McCord, Jr.—the committee's director of security.

Frederick C. LaRue—Mitchell's chief adviser.

Robert C. Mardian—another assistant to Mitchell.

director until March 1972, when John Mitchell resigned as attorney general to take over the job. Magruder remained on the reelection committee staff until March 1973, when he left for a position in the Commerce Department.

Election campaigns require money as well as organization, and Nixon was determined not to risk defeat through lack of money. Although he had more than one and a half million dollars left from his 1968 campaign, Nixon had his personal lawyer, Herbert Kalmbach, collect additional money throughout his first term as president. In February 1972, Maurice Stans resigned as commerce secretary to head the reelection committee's fundraising operations.

Stans's efforts were complicated by a new campaign financing law that took effect on April 7, 1972. The new law required the identification of most campaign contributions, something many contributors wanted to avoid. Stans rushed to bring in as much money as possible before that date. He received so many promises of campaign contributions as the deadline approached that some of the money failed to reach the committee in time. Moreover, some of the money that Stans raised came from corporations, a practice that the old law prohibited.

Nixon hoped to win reelection by dividing the Democrats and inducing them to nominate their weakest candidate. To accomplish this, he decided to wage an aggressive campaign involving the use of what he later described as "imaginative dirty tricks"—tricks such as those he believed the Democrats had used against him in the past.[1] For example, Nixon and other Republicans suspected that his narrow loss to Kennedy in 1960 was due to widespread voter fraud in Illinois and Texas.

BLACK BAGS, GEMSTONES, AND OTHER "DIRTY TRICKS." The first detailed plan for political dirty tricks was proposed in the summer of 1971 by Jack Caulfield, an assistant to White House counsel John Dean. Dean had come to the White House from the Justice Department in 1970 on Krogh's recommendation. Caulfield's plan, given the code name Sandwedge, borrowed many of the ideas that Tom Huston had proposed a year earlier. It called for several ways of spying on the Democrats, one of which was "black bag capability," a code phrase used by intelligence operatives to refer to break-ins, usually for the purpose of installing listening devices called bugs.

Caulfield also proposed gathering derogatory information on the Democrats, suggesting that the Internal Revenue Service files would be a useful source of such information. (Actually the Nixon administration had been using the IRS and other federal agencies to reward friends and punish enemies since Nixon's first days in office.)

In January 1972, Gordon Liddy, who had recently joined the reelection committee as its legal counsel, proposed a more comprehensive plan for political dirty tricks to replace Sandwedge, which had not been approved. Liddy outlined his plan, called Gemstone, during a meeting with Mitchell, Magruder, and Dean.

Liddy suggested a number of undercover activities, each with the code name of a gem. Many were wildly impractical. Later, after a discussion with Magruder, Liddy scaled down his plans, concentrating on placing undercover agents in Democratic campaign organizations and placing bugs in the offices of leading Democrats, particularly the Democratic National Committee headquarters and the presidential nominee's offices in Washington and Miami Beach, where the Democratic National Convention was to be held. Electronic surveillance to obtain political information clearly could not be justified on grounds of national security. Nevertheless, at Colson's urgings, the operation was approved after Magruder discussed it with Mitchell and Mitchell's aide, Frederick C. LaRue, on March 30, 1972.

Liddy's Gemstone activities were financed with reelection campaign funds. Magruder, with Mitchell's approval, authorized the payments to Liddy from a large supply of cash kept in the reelection committee's office. Magruder also regularly reported on Liddy's activities to

Gordon Strachan, Haldeman's principal political assistant, who was Haldeman's liaison with the reelection committee. Many of the political dirty tricks were directed against the campaign of Senator Edmund Muskie of Maine, who was the leading Democratic contender in 1971 and early 1972. Stopping Muskie from winning the nomination was important to Nixon because polls showed that Muskie and Nixon were almost tied for voter support. The tactics for interfering with Muskie's campaign included sending unordered food and drink to Muskie's fund-raising functions and distributing fake campaign literature, as well as planting spies in his campaign organization.

In April 1972, Muskie dropped out of the race after losing in the Wisconsin and Florida primaries, making Senator George McGovern of South Dakota the leading Democratic contender. (Muskie's poor showing in these elections may have been due as much to his own shortcomings as to Republican dirty tricks, however. Muskie often displayed outbursts of emotion during public speeches. He also tended to indulge in long, boring explanations of unimportant issues.)

THE WATERGATE BREAK-IN AND ARRESTS. Nixon and his supporters had long regarded McGovern, whose support came primarily from antiwar activists and other youthful protest groups, as the easiest Democrat to defeat. They were anxious to avoid a campaign against a popular, personable candidate with a broad appeal to the bulk of American voters. Such a candidate—Senator John F. Kennedy—had defeated Nixon in 1960. Nixon hoped to steer the Democrats into nominating someone the voters were likely to reject as too politically extreme. McGovern appeared to fit this image perfectly.

Senator Edmund Muskie of Maine was the target of Nixon's "dirty" campaign tricks. Although a leading Democratic contender in 1971, Muskie dropped out of the race in 1972.

The Nixon supporters were taking no chances, however. After Muskie failed to win in Wisconsin, Liddy shifted his intelligence operations from Muskie to the McGovern campaign organization. Liddy also continued his plans for the bugging of Democratic campaign offices, including McGovern's campaign headquarters in Washington.

Liddy's attempts to break into McGovern's office failed, but during Memorial Day weekend, a team of Liddy's men installed a listening device in the Democratic National Committee headquarters in a Washington hotel, apartment, and office complex called Watergate. (The buildings were so named because they were located near the Watergate, where the Potomac River flows into the Tidal Basin.) Liddy's men learned nothing that would be useful to the reelection campaign from the conversations they overheard, however.

On June 6, 1972, McGovern won the California primary, virtually assuring him of the Democratic nomination. A poll taken shortly thereafter showed Nixon with a commanding lead over McGovern. At that point the re-election committee might have discontinued its illegal activities as unnecessary risks. It did not, however. Instead, for reasons that have never been entirely clear, Liddy's men attempted another burglary of the Democrats' Watergate offices, with fateful results for the Nixon administration.

Early on Saturday morning, June 17, 1972, five of Liddy's men broke into these offices, bringing with them lock-picking tools, surgical gloves, photographic equipment, various listening devices, and over $2,000 in new $100 bills. Four of the burglars were Miami residents, some of whom had CIA connections. (Two of the four had taken part in the burglary of Dr. Fielding's office in 1971.) The fifth man was James McCord, a former CIA official who had been hired as director of security for the Republican National Committee and the Nixon reelection committee in January 1972. Before the burglars could complete their work, Washington police officers, alerted by a security guard, surprised and arrested them.

THE WATERGATE BURGLARY TEAM

The Burglars:
Bernard L. Barker—friend of E. Howard Hunt. Recruited other Miami residents for the break-in. Also took part in the burglary of Dr. Louis Fielding's office in 1971.
Virgilio R. Gonzalez—a locksmith from Miami.
Eugenio Rolando Martinez—a Cuban with ties to the CIA. Also took part in the burglary of Dr. Fielding's office.
James W. McCord, Jr.—a former CIA official and director of security for the Nixon reelection committee.
Frank A. Sturgis—an American citizen who fought in Cuba as a soldier of fortune.

The Lookout:
Alfred C. Baldwin—a former FBI employee, who watched the burglary from a nearby motel room.

The Leader:
G. Gordon Liddy—member of the Plumbers and director of security for the Nixon reelection committee.

Another of Liddy's men watched from a motel room across the street from the Democratic headquarters. The lookout reported the arrest to Hunt and Liddy, who were waiting in a room in the Watergate Hotel. The three men then vacated the rented rooms, leaving behind a mass of incriminating evidence.

After the arrest, the Washington police, suspecting that the break-in involved violations of federal laws, notified the U.S. attorney's office and the FBI. Fingerprints quickly revealed the identity of the men, all of whom had given fake names for the hotel register and to the police. McCord's connections with the CIA and the Republican organizations were also uncovered, and before much longer, the FBI had evidence connecting Hunt and Liddy to the burglary. The results of the preliminary investigation were turned over to a federal grand jury for consideration of criminal charges against those involved in the break-in.

As information on the break-in became public, both the White House and the reelection committee denied any knowledge of it. Actually, several of Nixon's top aides knew about Liddy's Gemstone operation, whether or not they were aware of all its details. Moreover, within a few days of the break-in, several others learned about Hunt's and Liddy's involvement in it.

A few hours after leaving the Watergate Hotel, Liddy telephoned Magruder, who was in California, to tell him what had happened. Magruder passed this information along to Mitchell and two of Mitchell's reelection committee aides, Frederick LaRue and Robert Mardian, a former assistant attorney general. Liddy later tried to get William Kleindienst, Mitchell's successor as attorney general, to arrange for the burglars' release from jail before their identities were learned. Kleindienst refused, but never reported what he knew to those who were investigating the break-in. His failure to do so could have resulted in his being charged with obstruction of justice. He was not charged with this crime, however, because the story of Liddy's discussion with him on this matter was not disclosed until much later.

On June 18, Magruder telephoned Haldeman to tell him about McCord's involvement in the break-in. On June 19, Liddy told Dean that the burglars were his men and that Magruder had wanted a second break-in because the reelection committee was not getting enough information on the Democrats as a result of the earlier break-in. Dean relayed this information to Ehrlichman and Colson.

On June 19, during a routine meeting with White House reporters, Nixon's press secretary, Ron Ziegler, dismissed the Watergate break-in as "a third-rate burglary attempt" not worth discussing. Actually, the administration was very much concerned over the break-in, which could lead to the discovery of Gemstone and the Nixon administration's other illegal activities. Such a discovery might result in Nixon's defeat in November—something that had to be prevented from happening. Magruder later wrote, in his book *An American Life: One Man's Road to Watergate,* that a cover-up was "immediate and automatic; no one ever considered that there would not be a cover-up."[2]

THE COVER-UP. One of the first steps in the cover-up was a massive destruction of documents. Among the documents destroyed were Magruder's and Liddy's Gemstone files, pages in the White House directory listing Hunt as a consultant, and papers in Haldeman's files showing that he knew about Gemstone. At Ehrlichman's suggestion, Hunt's White House safe was opened and its contents stashed away for safekeeping. In addition to a briefcase

Patrick Gray, appointed by Nixon in 1972 as acting director of the Federal Bureau of Investigation, received and later burned incriminating documents pertaining to the cover-up.

containing electronic equipment, Hunt's safe contained memoranda regarding the activities of the Plumbers, material regarding the Pentagon Papers, and forged State Department documents implicating the Kennedy administration in a political assassination in Vietnam. Some of this material was turned over to the FBI agents who were investigating the break-in. The more incriminating papers were later given to Patrick Gray, the acting director of the FBI, whom Nixon had appointed after Hoover's death in May 1972. Gray eventually burned them.

The Nixon administration also tried to keep the investigation of the Watergate burglary as much as possible under White House control. Dean, whom Nixon named as the White House liaison with the FBI and other Justice Department officials in the Watergate investigation, sat in on all FBI interviews with White House personnel. In some cases, he coached them beforehand to make sure their stories didn't reveal any wrongdoings. (Attorneys for the re-election committee also sat in on interviews with committee personnel.) Dean persuaded both Gray and Henry Petersen, the Justice Department official in charge of its criminal investigation division, to keep him informed of any new evidence that turned up. Petersen also agreed to keep the grand jury investigation limited to the break-in itself and away from other areas of inquiry.

In a press conference on August 29, 1972, Nixon referred to Dean's activities as a complete investigation that showed that no one then employed in his administration was involved in what he described as a "very bizarre incident." This was not Nixon's first denial of White House involvement. In a press conference on June 22, 1972, Nixon said, "The White House has no involvement whatever in this particular incident."

One significant disclosure that Gray made to Dean concerned the money found on the burglars. The FBI learned that it was part of a large cash withdrawal from one burglar's Miami bank account. The same burglar had also deposited five checks totalling more than $100,000 into his account. The checks were part of an attempt to "launder" Nixon campaign contributions (some of which were illegal), that is, create a series of financial transactions to conceal the original source of the money.

Dean reported this latest news to Haldeman, who discussed the matter with Nixon. Haldeman then arranged for the CIA to ask the FBI to refrain from further investigation into the source of the checks. The FBI was to be told that the money was connected with a CIA undercover operation, which, if disclosed, might harm national security. Magruder and one of his assistants later gave false testimony before the Watergate grand jury to cover up the payments Liddy received from the reelection campaign funds.

The only remaining problem was the possibility that one of the men involved in the burglary would tell his story to the prosecutors in the hope of either avoiding prosecution or receiving a lenient sentence. The Nixon aides handled this problem by making a series of undercover payments to the men to ensure their silence. The payments, which were made through third parties from campaign funds, were accompanied by promises of executive clemency—something that only the president had the authority to grant. Executive clemency is the president's power to grant reprieves and pardons for offenses against the United States, as provided by the Constitution.

THE ELECTION. On September 15, 1972, the grand jury indicted Hunt, Liddy, and the five Watergate burglars for illegal wiretapping and other related offenses. The seven pleaded not guilty, and their trial was set for November 15—after the election. (The trial was later postponed until January 1973.)

After the issuance of the indictments, the Justice Department announced that it had completed its investigation and had no evidence indicating that others should be charged with crimes.

The Democrats tried their best to make Watergate a campaign issue. The Democratic National Committee sued the reelection committee over the break-in. McGovern repeatedly brought up Watergate during his campaign

Washington Post *journalists Bob Woodward
and Carl Bernstein revealed much about the Watergate
scandal in their prize-winning investigative reporting.*

speeches. The *Washington Post,* a staunch opponent of the Nixon administration, printed numerous stories of developments regarding the break-in and its connection with Nixon's reelection campaign. (Two of its reporters, Bob Woodward and Carl Bernstein, did extensive investigating to uncover these stories. They later wrote two best-selling books describing their investigations, one of which was made into a movie.)

Despite these efforts, however, the voters showed little interest in the burglary. On November 7, 1972, Nixon was reelected, winning over 60 percent of the popular vote and every electoral vote except those of Massachusetts and the District of Columbia. Nixon still had a Democratic Congress, however—one that was, if anything, more hostile to him than the previous Congress had been.

8

THE WATERGATE COVER-UP FALLS APART

In January 1973, President Nixon finally fulfilled one of his 1968 campaign promises—getting the United States out of the war in Vietnam after eight years during which American military personnel fought in a losing cause. After Nixon's announcement of an agreement with North Vietnam to end the fighting, his approval rating in public opinion polls reached its highest point since 1969. The Nixon administration, however, was beginning to unravel.

On January 8, 1973, the trial of the seven Watergate defendants began in Washington's federal district court. The presiding judge was John J. Sirica, whose reputation for imposing harsh sentences on convicted criminals had earned him the nickname "Maximum John," referring to his issuance of maximum sentences.

Shortly after the start of the trial, five of the seven (all except Liddy and McCord) changed their pleas from innocent to guilty. The five men insisted that no one had tried to make them plead guilty and that no one else was involved in the break-in. After the jury convicted Liddy

Chief District Court Judge John J. Sirica, also known as
"Maximum John," presided over the trial of Hunt, Liddy,
and the five Watergate burglars.

and McCord, the judge scheduled sentencing for all of the
defendants for March 23.

Top Nixon administration officials had been afraid
for some time that Hunt, who had been demanding more
and more hush money, would tell his story in court. It was
McCord, however, who blew the lid off the Watergate
cover-up. During the sentencing hearing, Judge Sirica read
a letter McCord had written to him a couple of days earlier. The letter claimed that the defendants had been pres-

sured to plead guilty and remain silent, that perjury had been committed during the trial, and that others had been involved in the burglary. After postponing McCord's sentencing, the judge sentenced Liddy, who had been uncooperative throughout the trial, to twenty years in prison. He then imposed harsh provisional sentences on the other defendants with a promise to review the sentences after the men had an opportunity to provide additional information about the break-in. (Later that year Sirica substantially reduced these sentences.)

CONFESSIONS AND RESIGNATIONS. On March 26, 1973, the grand jury that had heard the original Watergate charges reconvened to hear further testimony. The prosecutors wanted particularly to hear McCord's testimony, but they had to wait a while. First, McCord told his story to a Senate select committee headed by Senator Sam Ervin of North Carolina, a folksy Southerner who was fond of quoting the Bible and Shakespeare. The committee was organized in February 1973 to investigate the 1972 election campaign activities, including the Watergate break-in.

Much of McCord's knowledge was only secondhand, gleaned from his conversations with Liddy. His statements were damaging to the Nixon administration, however. McCord claimed that Magruder had lied in his trial testimony and that both Magruder and Dean had known about the Watergate break-in. McCord also implicated Colson and Mitchell, both of whom had left the Nixon administration sometime earlier, in the burglary and its cover-up.

When McCord gave his information to the Ervin committee, another Senate committee, the Judiciary Committee, was interested in hearing from Dean. In February 1973, Nixon nominated L. Patrick Gray to be the FBI's permanent director, a position that required Senate confirmation.

During the Senate Judiciary Committee's confirmation hearings, Gray revealed his dealings with Dean during the initial Watergate investigation. Dean managed to avoid testifying before the Judiciary Committee, but after learning about McCord's revelations to the Ervin committee, Dean decided he had better make the best deal he could to minimize, or possibly escape, punishment. He hired a lawyer and began talking to the federal prosecutors.

Magruder, who was then working for the Commerce Department, also revealed his part in the Watergate affair. Magruder had also consulted lawyers, who advised him to tell the whole story to the prosecutors in the hope of receiving lenient treatment. In a meeting with the Watergate prosecutors on April 14, 1973, Magruder admitted his own role in both Operation Gemstone (which led to the Watergate break-in) and the subsequent cover-up. He also implicated Dean, Ehrlichman, Mitchell, Mardian, and La Rue. On April 26, Magruder resigned from his Commerce Department position.

Several other high-level Nixon aides left their jobs later that month. Gray resigned after disclosing that he had destroyed Hunt's files. (Gray claimed that when he was given this material, he got the impression from Ehrlichman and Dean that the president wanted it to be destroyed.) Shortly before the end of the month, Ehrlichman and Haldeman resigned at Nixon's request after the president learned that Magruder and Dean had linked both men to the Watergate break-in and the cover-up. At the same time Kleindienst resigned at Nixon's request. Finally, Nixon fired Dean after learning that Dean had threatened to implicate him as well as Haldeman, Ehrlichman, and Mitchell if he was brought to trial for Watergate-related offenses.

On April 30, 1973, in announcing the resignations and the firing of Dean, the president said that new information had convinced him that despite their repeated statements to the contrary, there was a real possibility that members of his staff had been involved in the Watergate affair. Nixon then announced the appointment of his defense secretary, Elliott Richardson, as attorney general, adding that he had given Richardson absolute authority to make decisions regarding Watergate and related matters.

Dean's discussions with the Watergate prosecutors in April 1973 reopened the Daniel Ellsberg affair. In mid-April, Dean revealed that Hunt and Liddy had been involved in the 1971 burglary of Ellsberg's psychiatrist's office. At the time of Dean's disclosure, Ellsberg was on trial for the theft of the Pentagon Papers. The Ellsberg prosecutors tried to give this information to the trial judge privately, but the judge disclosed it in open court. He also asked for a complete report on the information in the government's files regarding Ellsberg.

Shortly after Ellsberg's 1971 indictment, Mardian, who was then the Justice Department official responsible for overseeing the case, asked the FBI whether its files contained any wiretap information on Ellsberg. The request was a routine effort to locate information that might have to be given to the defense attorneys—a process known as discovery. The FBI reported that it had no information on Ellsberg. This was not completely true. Although Ellsberg's telephone had not been tapped, the special files on the Kissinger taps contained reports on several of Ellsberg's conversations with a National Security Council official whose telephone had been tapped.

After the judge asked for an updated report on the Ellsberg case, the FBI disclosed that it had obtained wiretap information on him, but that the records of the wiretapped conversations were missing. (They were later found with Ehrlichman's White House papers. They had been delivered to Ehrlichman shortly after Mardian had asked about FBI wiretap information on Ellsberg.) When the judge learned about the missing wiretap reports, he denounced the government's conduct and dismissed the charges against Ellsberg.

PUBLIC HEARINGS AND TESTIMONY AGAINST THE PRESIDENT. On May 17, 1973, the Ervin committee began its public hearings, which were carried on national television. Five days later, in a national address, the president denied any knowledge of the Watergate break-in, its subsequent cover-up, or any payment to the Watergate defendants. He also denied authorizing any offer of executive clemency to these men or any attempt to implicate the CIA in the Watergate affair. He did, however, acknowledge instructing Haldeman and Ehrlichman to make sure that the investigation of the break-in did not expose the actions of the Special Investigations Unit (the Plumbers) concerning national security.

The president's public denials were not enough to counteract the evidence presented against him during the Ervin committee's public hearings. McCord and Jack Caulfield testified regarding the offers of executive clemency to the Watergate defendants before they went on trial. Maurice Stans and the reelection committee treasurer, Hugh W. Sloan, Jr., testified about the payments to Liddy from Nixon's campaign funds. Magruder testified regarding his own part in Operation Gemstone and the involvement of other reelection committee and White House officials in the Watergate burglary and the cover-up. Dean spent four days describing the Nixon administration's political dirty tricks: wiretaps, burglaries, money-laundering, spying, the 1970 Huston Plan for controlling subversive activities (which became the basis for these dirty tricks), the Plumbers, the Watergate cover-up, and the attempts to obstruct

Senator Sam Ervin of North Carolina (far right) was chairman of the Senate Watergate Committee. Here he confers with committee members and staff: (from left to right) Senator Howard Baker of Tennessee, Senator Lowell Weicker of Connecticut, assistant counsel Terry Lenzer, and assistant counsel Rufus Edmisten.

the operations of federal agencies. Dean also testified that Nixon was directly involved in the offers of executive clemency and the payment of hush money to Hunt.

THE TAPES. Mitchell, Haldeman, and Ehrlichman tried their best to defend themselves and Nixon before the Ervin committee. The testimony of Haldeman and Ehrlichman was anticlimactic, however. On Friday, July 13, 1973 (a very unlucky day for Nixon), a former White House aide,

Alexander Butterfield, surprised the Ervin committee staff by mentioning that most of the president's conversations were on tape. Butterfield thought the committee already knew about the automatic taping system Nixon had ordered for several of his offices early in 1971. Immediately after Butterfield's revelation, Nixon's new White House chief of staff, Alexander Haig, had the taping system shut down and the tapes moved to a safer location. He and several other Nixon advisers also discussed whether or not to destroy them. Some recommended the destruction of this potentially damaging evidence against the president. Others objected because the destruction of evidence that could be used in a criminal trial was itself a criminal offense, which, if discovered, would undoubtedly lead to Nixon's impeachment. Nixon decided not to destroy the tapes—a decision he later had reason to regret.

Butterfield's public testimony regarding the White House taping system resulted in a lengthy battle for access to the tapes.The Ervin committee issued legal demands called subpoenas for several tapes. So did Archibald Cox, the special prosecutor whom Richardson had appointed in May to investigate Watergate in response to the Senate's unanimous recommendation. The Senate wanted a lawyer with authority independent of the Justice Department to investigate this matter and bring those guilty of crimes to justice. A special prosecutor would serve this purpose.

Nixon refused to release the tapes. His lawyers argued that they related to private conversations between the president and members of his immediate staff. Their release could interfere with a president's right to the confidential advice of his subordinates. This doctrine, called executive privilege, was an important part of the ensuing controversy regarding the tapes. Cox responded to this ar-

John D. Ehrlichman testifying before the Senate Watergate Committee denied that Nixon had granted executive clemency for the seven Watergate conspirators.

gument by stating that the president has no constitutional power to withhold evidence from a grand jury, which occupies a fundamental position in the administration of public justice.

On August 29, 1973, Judge Sirica ruled that Nixon must make certain tapes available to him for his private review of their relevance to the grand jury investigation. Both Cox and Nixon appealed this ruling. (Nixon did not want to release the tapes at all, while Cox wanted to examine the tapes himself instead of relying on Sirica's decisions regarding their relevance.)

On October 12, 1973, after its suggestion of an out-of-court compromise failed to bring an agreement, the U.S. Appeals Court upheld Sirica's order.

MORE SCANDAL, RESIGNATIONS, AND FIRINGS. After the appeals court upheld Judge Sirica's order regarding the tapes, Nixon again tried to avoid releasing them. He offered to submit written transcripts to Sirica after Senator John Stennis of Mississippi (a conservative Democrat who strongly supported Nixon) verified their contents. (Stennis, who was hard of hearing, was not exactly a good choice as someone to listen to these tapes, which were of very poor quality and hard to understand.) Nixon also insisted that Cox make no demands for additional tapes. When Cox refused to agree to either the acceptance of written transcripts instead of the tapes themselves or a limit on his ability to examine additional tapes, Nixon asked Richardson to fire Cox. Richardson refused, citing his promise to the Senate Judiciary Committee in May that he alone would have the authority to fire Cox, and then only for serious improprieties, which he did not believe Cox had committed. Richardson and his deputy, William Ruckelshaus, then resigned. Robert Bork, the U.S. solicitor general (the third

SPIRO T. AGNEW

The scandal concerning Nixon's administration continued to widen. On October 10, 1973, Vice President Spiro T. Agnew resigned after pleading "no contest" to a charge of income tax evasion. Agnew, who would have become president on Nixon's impeachment and conviction, may have saved Nixon from impeachment earlier in the year. At the end of July, Democratic Representative Robert Drinan of Massachusetts had introduced an impeachment resolution. No action was taken on it, however. The House's failure to act may have been at least partly due to the Democrats' reluctance to have Agnew, who had indulged in what they regarded as unfair attacks on them during election campaigns, succeed to the presidency.

highest-ranking Justice Department official), agreed to fire Cox and to assume Richardson's duties until a permanent attorney general was selected.

On Saturday evening, October 20, 1973, in an action that became known as the Saturday Night Massacre, Nixon's press secretary announced that Cox and Ruckelshaus had been fired, Richardson had resigned, and Bork had been appointed acting attorney general. He also announced the abolition of the office of special prosecutor, saying that the Watergate investigation would be

handled by the Justice Department's regular staff. A few days later, Bork put Henry Petersen, who had cooperated with the White House during the initial Watergate investigation, in charge of further investigations.

Nixon believed that as Richardson's superior he had the legal authority to fire Cox regardless of any agreement to the contrary. Most people thought the attorney general had to do the firing, but Bork, who fired Cox, thought the president could fire Cox himself. Nixon's action, however, resulted in a deluge of protest from Americans who saw it as an attempt to defy the court. A number of bills were introduced in Congress calling for the appointment of a new special prosecutor. Several members of the House of Representatives introduced resolutions calling for Nixon's impeachment. (One was Representative Lud Ashley of

Ohio, the great-grandson of Representative James Ashley, who had called for Andrew Johnson's impeachment in 1867.) The impeachment resolutions were referred to the House Judiciary Committee for further action.

On October 23, Nixon agreed to surrender the subpoenaed tapes to Judge Sirica. Nixon's action was too late to stop action on the impeachment resolutions, however. On that same day Representative Peter Rodino of New Jersey, who headed the Judiciary Committee, announced that the committee would move ahead with an impeachment investigation. In making his announcement, Rodino noted that the president's actions had raised serious questions about the integrity of the government and the administration of the nation's justice system.

9

PRESIDENT NIXON
RESIGNS

Shortly after agreeing to give Judge Sirica the tapes that
Cox had subpoenaed, President Nixon agreed to the ap-
pointment of another special prosecutor. Acting Attorney
General Bork named a prominent Texas lawyer, Leon
Jaworski.

Before Jaworski began work, a new problem arose
concerning the tapes. On October 30, 1973, Nixon's lawyers informed Judge Sirica privately that two of the conversations Cox wanted to review had not been recorded.
These were a telephone conversation between Nixon and
Mitchell on June 20, 1972, and a discussion between Nixon
and Dean on April 15, 1973. (It was subsequently learned
that a recording of the president's personal notes on the
April 15 meeting was also missing.) In November, Nixon's
lawyers reported that another tape contained a segment of
eighteen and a half minutes during which only a loud hum
could be heard. This tape dealt with a meeting between
Nixon and Haldeman on June 20, 1972. (According to
Haldeman's notes, the missing segment contained a dis-

*Houston attorney and past president of the
American Bar Association, Leon Jaworski was
appointed as special Watergate prosecutor.*

cussion of the Watergate break-in.) The president's personal secretary, Rose Mary Woods, explained that she had accidentally erased part of the tape while transcribing its contents, but few believed her. A panel of experts later reported that the gap was the result of a series of manual erasures that could not have occurred by accident.

The first report on the missing tapes led to a number of requests for Nixon's resignation. Some of these requests came from newspapers that had previously supported the president, and one came from Senator Edward Brooke of Massachusetts, the first Republican in Congress to make such a suggestion. At that point Nixon's resignation would have made a Democrat, House Speaker Carl Albert, president of the United States. Since there was no vice president, Albert was next in line for the presidency under the rules of succession that were in effect in 1973. This potential problem for the Republicans was resolved in December 1973, when Congress confirmed Republican Representative Gerald Ford of Michigan as vice president. This was done under a provision of the Twenty-Fifth Amendment, which authorized the filling of a vacancy in the office of vice president by a president's nomination and its confirmation by a majority of both houses of Congress.

WHAT WAS ON THE TAPES. After receiving the subpoenaed tapes and deleting material that did not pertain to Watergate, Sirica gave them to the Watergate prosecutors. The first tape the prosecutors played involved a meeting that Nixon had with Dean and Haldeman on March 21, 1973 (two days before the initial sentencing of the Watergate burglars). Dean had previously testified before the Ervin committee concerning that meeting. He had stated that during the meeting he told the president about Gemstone and the Watergate cover-up, including Magruder's perjury, the payment of hush money, and the need for more money. The tape corroborated Dean's testimony. It revealed that Nixon agreed that Hunt's demands for more hush money must be met and that he said a million dollars could be obtained to pay off the Watergate defendants.

The March 21, 1973, tape also recorded a discussion of the question of who could avoid criminal liability—a discussion in which Nixon told Haldeman to respond to questions by saying, "I don't remember." After listening to this tape, Jaworski suggested to Haig that the president hire a criminal lawyer. Nixon later hired a prominent Boston trial lawyer, James St. Clair, to handle his Watergate defense. By that time, Nixon himself must have been worried about possible criminal charges. On November 17, 1973, Nixon blurted out on national television, "Well, I am not a crook."

The tapes Jaworski had received provided evidence against others as well as against the president. On March 1, 1974, the grand jury indicted seven Nixon aides— Mitchell, Haldeman, Ehrlichman, Colson, Mardian, Strachan, and a reelection committee lawyer, Kenneth Parkinson—for conspiracy to obstruct justice and for other offenses in connection with the Watergate break-in. It also gave Sirica a secret report in which it named Nixon as an unindicted co-conspirator (a person the grand jury has evidence against but whom it declines to charge with a crime). The grand jury also recommended that its evidence be given to the House Judiciary Committee for use in the impeachment investigation. On March 26, 1974, Sirica complied with the grand jury's request.

After the indictment of the seven Nixon aides, both the House Judiciary Committee and Jaworski demanded additional tapes of the president's conversations. In April 1974, Nixon released to the public edited transcripts of

Nixon's White House chief of staff, Alexander Haig.

more than forty tapes, claiming that they told the whole story of the Watergate affair. The transcripts further damaged Nixon's reputation, which was already at a low point following the revelations of the missing and altered tapes. Many of the president's remarks had been taken out of the transcripts and the phrase "expletive deleted" inserted in their place. The public assumed that these deletions referred to vulgar, offensive, or obscene language. Other deletions made on the grounds that the deleted passages were unrelated to Watergate were even more damaging, because they gave the impression of a White House cover-up.

Nixon hoped that by releasing the transcripts he would avoid having to release the tapes themselves. However, the edited transcripts failed to satisfy either the House Judiciary Committee or Jaworski. After Jaworski subpoenaed sixty-four additional tapes, James St. Clair claimed that the prosecutors already had all the evidence they needed for the trial of Nixon's aides. He also argued that executive privilege protected the president from having to release the tapes.

St. Clair's arguments failed to sway Judge Sirica, who ordered the president to obey the subpoena. St. Clair then asked the appeals court to review Sirica's order. Jaworski, however, asked the Supreme Court to rule on the issue without waiting for the decision of the appeals court. On May 31 the Court agreed to review the matter and scheduled a hearing for July 8.

PREPARING FOR IMPEACHMENT. Meanwhile, on May 9 the House Judiciary Committee began holding hearings on the president's impeachment in closed sessions. Several preliminary steps had already been taken on this matter. John M. Doar, a former Justice Department prosecutor, had been hired as special counsel to handle the impeachment inquiry.

Doar and his staff had compiled a massive list of evidence of the activities of the president and his aides in a number of areas, including the Watergate cover-up, undercover intelligence operations, the use of federal agencies for political purposes, the president's personal finances, and his conduct of the war in Vietnam. In compiling this evidence, Doar's staff had access to the records of the Ervin committee, the Watergate grand jury, and the criminal and civil trials that had already taken place. It also had some of the president's tapes.

Part of the inquiry staff's investigation involved the issue of what actions were grounds for impeachment. Nixon's attorneys had argued, much as Andrew Johnson's attorneys had argued more than a century earlier, that the president could be impeached only for criminal offenses. After extensive research into the history of American impeachments, the staff concluded that impeachable offenses were not limited to crimes, but could include serious misconduct in office.

As explained in Chapter 1, the framers of the Constitution generally believed that impeachment was justified for political offenses such as an abuse of an officeholder's public trust or of his legitimate powers. In its report on the results of its research the staff commented: "In short, the framers who discussed impeachment in the state ratifying conventions, as well as other delegates who favored the Constitution, implied that it reached offenses against the government, and especially abuses of constitutional duties. The opponents did not argue that the grounds for impeachment had been limited to criminal offenses."[1]

Doar believed, however, that impeachment should not be based on one particular action, whether criminal or not. Accordingly, he focused on the Nixon administration's

" I GOT IT FROM AN IMPEACHABLE SOURCE"

entire record, which he believed showed a pattern of misconduct serious enough to warrant Nixon's impeachment.

After Doar presented his evidence, the committee called several witnesses to testify before it. St. Clair then presented the president's case, while Doar and other attorneys presented the arguments for and against impeachment. By the middle of July, Doar's staff had begun to draft specific charges against the president for the committee's consideration.

FURTHER COMPLICATIONS. While the House committee was winding up its closed sessions and preparing for public hearings, other events further damaged the president's credibility. In June the grand jury report naming him as an unindicted co-conspirator in the Watergate cover-up was leaked to the public. The Ervin committee's final report, issued on June 30, 1974, provided further evidence of the Nixon administration's improper conduct. The House Judiciary Committee also released its own transcripts of the Nixon tapes, showing that Nixon's edited transcripts omitted material that did not agree with his public statements.

The July hearings before the Supreme Court on the subpoena of the president's tapes centered on the question of executive privilege. On July 24, 1974, the Court held that a president could withhold confidential information on grounds of executive privilege. Such privilege could not be invoked to withhold evidence in a criminal trial, however. The Court therefore ruled that Nixon must give the sixty-four subpoenaed tapes to Judge Sirica for his private review of what portions could be withheld as privileged communications. Eight justices, four of whom were Nixon appointees, joined in the decision. The ninth justice, William Rehnquist, who had served in the Justice Department during the Nixon administration, declined to participate in it to avoid any suggestion that he had a conflict of interest.

When the Court announced its ruling, an anxious nation waited to see what the president would do. The atmosphere of tension was similar to the atmosphere more than a hundred years earlier when the House debated the impeachment of President Andrew Johnson. Would Nixon defy the Court despite his earlier promise to abide by a definitive Supreme Court ruling? If so, how could the Court or Congress compel his obedience? He was, after all, commander in chief of the armed forces. What if he used them to force the other branches of government to take back their demands? At least one member of Nixon's cabinet was concerned about such a constitutional crisis. James Schlesinger, Nixon's secretary of defense, instructed all military commanders not to obey any orders from the White House that did not contain his signature.

The constitutional crisis failed to materialize, however, just as it had failed in 1868. That evening St. Clair announced that the president would comply with the Court's ruling.

THE SMOKING GUN. While St. Clair was making his announcement, the House Judiciary Committee was ready to start its public hearings on the articles of impeachment. The televised sessions began with a brief speech by each member of the committee. Afterward, the committee voted on each of the articles that Doar's staff had drafted. On July 27, 1974, the committee voted to accept the first article of impeachment, which charged the president with obstructing the administration of justice by his participation in the Watergate cover-up. The vote was 27 to 11 in favor of this article. Six of the committee's seventeen Republicans joined the twenty-one Democrats in supporting it. By that time, it was clear to the twenty-seven who had voted "aye" that the president had known about the Watergate break-in soon after it occurred and that he had lied repeatedly to cover up his staff's involvement in this crime.

Two days later the committee voted 28 to 10 to accept the second article of impeachment, which charged the

---

LIES AND MORE LIES

President Nixon's public statements:

June 22, 1972—". . . the White House press secretary, Ron Ziegler, had spoken accurately regarding the Watergate break-in in saying, 'The White House has no involvement whatever in this particular incident.'"

August 29, 1972—"I can say categorically that . . . no one in the White House staff, no one in this administration, presently employed, was involved in this very bizarre incident."

March 2, 1973—". . . no one on the White House staff . . . was involved or had knowledge of the Watergate matter."

March 15, 1973—"We will cooperate fully with the Senate, just as we did with the grand jury, as we did with the FBI, and as we did with the courts when they were conducting their investigations previously in what was called the Watergate matter."

April 17, 1973—"I condemn any attempts to cover up in this case, no matter who is involved."

> *April 30, 1973*—"Until March of this year I
> remained convinced that . . . the charges of involve-
> ment by members of the White House staff were
> false."
> *May 22, 1973*—"I took no part in, nor was I
> aware of, any subsequent efforts that may have been
> made to cover up Watergate. At no time did I autho-
> rize any offer of executive clemency for the
> Watergate defendants, nor did I know of any such
> offer. I did not know, until the time of my own in-
> vestigation, of any effort to provide the Watergate
> defendants with funds. At no time did I attempt, or
> did I authorize orders to attempt, to implicate the
> CIA in the Watergate matter . . . ."
> *August 15, 1973*—"I state again . . . I had no
> prior knowledge of the Watergate break-in; I neither
> took part in nor knew about any of the subsequent
> cover-up activities . . . ."

president with the misuse of his official power by interfering with federal agencies such as the IRS, the CIA, the
FBI, and other Justice Department components. On July
30, 1974, the committee voted 21 to 17 to accept the third
article of impeachment, which charged the president with
failure to comply with House subpoenas issued from April
through June 1974.

The committee rejected two additional articles, one
dealing with the president's concealment from Congress
of his 1970 orders for the bombing of Cambodian sites,
and the other dealing with the president's unlawful evasion of income taxes.

On August 2 the president's lawyer gave Judge Sirica the subpoenaed tapes. Three days later, the president released transcripts of three conversations that were included in the subpoenaed material. The conversations took place on June 23, 1972, less than a week after the Watergate break-in. During one conversation between Nixon and Haldeman, the two men discussed the possibility of getting the FBI to stop its investigation of the Watergate break-in by claiming that the burglary was part of a CIA operation involving national security. This tape, which became known as the "smoking gun" tape, revealed that the president had not only tried to obstruct justice but had lied to the American people for more than two years about his knowledge of the Watergate break-in. After its release, the president's remaining support among Republicans in Congress evaporated.

On August 8, 1974, following a meeting in which Republican congressional leaders told the president that he was sure to be impeached by the House and almost sure to be convicted by the Senate, Richard M. Nixon publicly resigned from office, and on August 9, Gerald Ford became president.

PARDON. On September 8, 1974, in an act that was widely condemned, President Ford gave Nixon a full pardon for any crimes committed while he was president. The condemnation was not unanimous, however. Some believed that because of the extensive publicity, Nixon could not have received a fair trial. Others argued that Nixon's humiliating removal from office was enough punishment.

Ford's action spared the nation from the embarrassment and turmoil of a possible indictment and trial of a former president. It also, however, prevented the full disclosure of the case against Nixon. One member of the House Judiciary Committee called the pardon "the ultimate cover-up."[2] Ford did not pardon any of Nixon's aides, however. Early in 1975, Mitchell, Haldeman, Ehrlichman, and Mardian were convicted of crimes stemming from the Watergate break-in. Parkinson, who apparently was never fully aware of the Watergate cover-up, was acquitted. The charges against Colson (who had already pleaded guilty to a conspiracy charge in connection with the Ellsberg case) and Strachan were dropped. Mardian's conviction was overturned on appeal. By the time the Watergate scandal played itself out, more than thirty of Nixon's aides, including Mitchell, Haldeman, Ehrlichman, Magruder, Dean, Hunt, and Liddy, had gone to prison for their part in the Nixon administration's illegal activities.

In accepting the 1968 Republican nomination for the presidency, Nixon had said, "Truth will become the hallmark of the Nixon administration." Nixon's subsequent conduct did not live up to that promise, however. When Doar recommended to the House Judiciary Committee in 1974 that Nixon be impeached, he told the committee that the charges against the president were essentially his "concealment, duplicity, dissembling."

President Ford touched on that same theme during his inaugural address when he said, "I believe that truth is the glue that holds governments together."[3]

THE LESSONS OF WATERGATE. The Watergate scandal prompted Congress to initiate a number of reforms. Even before President Nixon was driven from office, Congress tried to get a handle on his actions concerning the Vietnam War. In 1973, Congress passed the War Powers Resolution over the president's veto. This resolution, while recognizing the necessity for the president to order American armed forces into action in emergency situations, required him to report to Congress within forty-eight hours on any such use of military force, and to withdraw American troops if Congress refused to approve their continued presence in a war zone.

In the years following Nixon's resignation, Congress enacted several laws designed to correct the abuse of government powers that was so widespread during the Nixon administration. In response to Nixon's coercive and illegal fund-raising efforts during his 1972 reelection campaign, Congress attempted to tighten the rules regarding contributions to political campaigns. A 1974 law limited the amounts of money that contributors could give to any one candidate for public office, but loopholes in the law itself and subsequent Supreme Court decisions considerably weakened the law's effect. As a result, both wealthy individuals and political action committees can give large amounts of money to finance election campaigns in the hope of influencing the policies of a winning candidate for public office. Campaign finance reform remains an unsolved problem in American politics today.

Congress also tried to curb the misuse of the CIA's authority to conduct undercover activities. In 1974, Congress passed the Hughes-Ryan Amendment to the Foreign Assistance Act. The amendment required the president to approve all CIA undercover operations and report on them to Congress. The Foreign Intelligence Surveillance Act of 1978 required the CIA to get warrants from the attorney general before conducting surveillance activies within the United States. The Intelligence Oversight Act of 1980 required the CIA to report to Congress on its undercover activities.

Congress also considered curbs on the FBI's intelligence-gathering activities, but was unable to agree on any needed legislation. Various attorneys general have issued rules regarding the FBI's conduct of domestic security investigations, but concern about the FBI's possible abuse of its authority remains widespread today.

One of the most significant reforms resulting from Watergate was the creation of a permanent mechanism for the appointment of a special prosecutor to conduct a thorough investigation of suspected wrongdoing by high-level officials. In 1978, Congress passed the Ethics in Government Act. In addition to the establishment of procedures for appointing a special prosecutor (a term that was changed to independent counsel in 1983), this law required officials of the executive and judicial branches of the federal government (but not members of Congress) to file reports on their own financial situations. Congress hoped by this provision to prevent federal officials from entering into financial arrangements that conflicted with their responsibilities to the public.

All of these reform efforts were designed to reinforce what seemed at the time to be the central lesson of Watergate—the need for the nation's chief executive to be honest with the American people. However, only a little more than a decade elapsed before another scandal involving secret and possibly illegal activities by White House personnel threatened the administration of another American president—Ronald Reagan.

10

PRESIDENT RONALD REAGAN AND THE IRAN-*CONTRA* SCANDAL

Twelve years after President Nixon resigned, Americans learned about a new series of undercover dealings by White House aides that not only conflicted with the nation's stated foreign policy but also appeared to violate federal laws. The revelations caused many to wonder whether a second Watergate-type scandal was coming to light—a scandal that might result in the undoing of another American president, Ronald Reagan.

In November 1986 a Lebanese magazine reported that the United States had been secretly sending military equipment to Iran in violation of an American arms embargo against that country. The magazine article also stated that a group of Americans, including a former national security adviser, had met Iranian officials late that summer in Iran's capital city, Tehran, apparently to discuss further shipments of armaments.

The speaker of the Iranian parliament confirmed the magazine's report of the meeting, adding that there were also discussions at that meeting about the possibility of

Ronald Reagan (seated, at center), fortieth president of the United States, jokes with Vice President George Bush (far left). Defense Secretary Caspar Weinberger is seated at right.

Iranians helping to obtain the release of several American hostages being held by pro-Iranian terrorists in Lebanon. The terrorists had already freed one hostage in July 1986. They released another shortly after the publication of the magazine article. The timing of these incidents led many Americans to suspect that the arms shipments were a ransom for the release of the hostages.

THE HOSTAGE SITUATION. In 1979 a mob of Iranians had stormed the American embassy in Tehran, captured a number of American diplomatic and military personnel, and held them for more than a year. The Iranians were angry about continued American support of Shah Mohammed Reza Pahlavi, a right-wing dictator and long-term ally of the United States, whose regime in Iran had recently been overthrown. The mob action resulted in a break in American diplomatic relations with Iran, whose new leader, Ayatollah Ruhollah Khomeini, repeatedly called America the "Great Satan." Another result was an American ban on arms sales to Iran.

Shortly after the 1986 disclosure of the American arms shipments to Iran, an embarrassed President Reagan tried to explain matters in a nationally televised speech. The president denied any attempt to trade arms for the hostages that were at that time being held in Lebanon. He claimed that his administration had been trying to establish contact with moderate Iranians in the hope of restoring friendly relations with that country and keeping it from forming closer ties with the Soviet Union. The president's explanation was unconvincing, however. More than half of the American public believed that the Reagan administration, despite its repeated pledges never to pay ransom to terrorists, had agreed to send arms to a hostile country in exchange for the release of American hostages, as the speaker of the Iranian parliament had implied.

Matters worsened quickly. Less than a month after the initial disclosure of the arms deals, the Reagan administration announced that much of the money that Iran had paid for the military supplies had been diverted to support a group of rebels, called *contras,* who were carrying on guerrilla warfare against the Nicaraguan government.

This government had been formed in 1979, after Nicaraguan rebels ousted right-wing dictator Anastasio Somoza. At first the United States tried to help the rebel government, but this support weakened in the wake of reports of the increasing influence of Marxists in the new government and evidence that Nicaragua, with the assistance of the Communist government of Cuba, was providing military aid to left-wing rebels in nearby El Salvador. In 1981, President Reagan, fearing a Communist takeover of Central America, authorized the Central Intelligence Agency to provide financial support for the *contras* in an effort to disrupt the flow of arms to the Salvadoran rebels.

Congress initially went along with this, but in 1984, in response to increasing public worry that the United States was drifting into a replay of the Vietnam war, Congress specifically forbade the use of any federal money for attempts to overthrow the Nicaraguan government. This provision, introduced by representative Edward Boland, the chair of the House Intelligence Committee, became known as the Boland Amendment.

In his public statement on November 25, 1986, regarding what came to be known as the Iran-*contra* scandal, Attorney General Edwin Meese said that he had learned a day or so earlier that an official in the National Security Council, Marine Lieutenant Colonel Oliver North, was responsible for the diversion of funds to the *contras*. According to Meese, Colonel North had concealed the diversion from everyone except his immediate superior, Admiral John M. Poindexter, national security adviser. Meese then announced Admiral Poindexter's resignation and Colonel North's firing and promised to continue his investigation.

INVESTIGATING THE NSC COWBOYS AND THE CIA. Colonel North was part of a controversial group of National Security Council staff members officially called a crisis management team, but referred to by Washington insiders as the "cowboys" because of their habit of engaging in risky enterprises. (In this respect, the cowboys were not unlike

Marine Lieutenant Colonel Oliver North was responsible for the diversion of U.S. funds to support the contras, *a rebel group conducting guerilla warfare against the Nicaraguan government.*

the Nixon administration's Plumbers.) North, a decorated veteran of the Vietnam War, had been assigned to the NSC staff in 1981. While there, he had taken an active part in various undercover activities. He helped Robert C. McFarlane, Poindexter's predecessor as national security adviser, with the negotiations that led to the shipment of arms to Iran.

After Meese made his announcement, Reagan appointed a three-member commission to investigate the National Security Council's structure and role in American foreign policy. The commission was headed by former Republican Senator John Tower of Texas, who had previously headed the Senate Armed Services Committee. Its other members were former Senator Muskie, who had served as President Carter's secretary of state, and Brent Scowcroft, who had served as President Ford's national security adviser. At the same time, the Senate Intelligence Committee was investigating the CIA's role in funding the *contras.*

Both the Tower Commission and the Senate Intelligence Committee reports showed a White House riddled with dissension and suspicion, lacking in adequate supervision of subordinate staff, and headed by a president who seemed out of touch with the details of his administration's policies. Although sharply critical of the president, both reports concluded that the president had not known about the illegal use of federal funds to support the *contras.*

Meese's hasty investigation in November 1986 was widely criticized. Meese had allowed North to retain access to his files during the investigation, giving North and his secretary the opportunity to destroy a large number of documents relating to North's undercover activities. Some people thought Meese's investigation was actually an attempt to cover up the Reagan administration's involvement

DIVERTING FUNDS TO
HELP THE *CONTRAS*

The idea for the diversion grew out of a 1984 discussion between the president and retired Marine Lieutenant Colonel Robert C. McFarlane, who was then the president's national security adviser. (McFarlane left late in 1985 and was replaced by Poindexter.)

After passage of the 1984 Boland Amendment, with its ban on future aid to the *contras,* the president told McFarlane that he wanted this group to be kept functioning. McFarlane solicited money from foreign governments to help the Nicaraguan rebels, while his subordinate, North (who was a close friend of McFarlane), arranged for private groups to raise money from private citizens.

North then got CIA Director William J. Casey to furnish the names of arms dealers who could buy armaments for the *contras* with the money he and McFarlane raised. (Casey, who died in May 1987, never explained his role in this enterprise.) The government of Israel cooperated by selling arms it had obtained from the United States to Iran and depositing the proceeds of the sales in a secret Swiss bank account. North then arranged for the transfer to the *contras* of some of the profit from the sales.

Despite the Boland Act of 1984, which banned aid to the contras, *President Reagan and Robert McFarlane designed a plan to continue supporting the rebel group. North worked for McFarlane.*

in the scandal. Many Americans wondered whether both Reagan and Vice President George Bush had known about the diversion of funds from the arms sales to support the *contras.* Bush publicly denied any such knowledge, but suspicions remained regarding his role.

In December 1986 the Reagan adminstration agreed to the appointment of an independent counsel to look into the possibility of criminal charges based on the Iran-*contra* affair. (The position of independent counsel, which had been authorized by the Ethics in Government Act of 1978, was an outgrowth of the Watergate scandal.) A panel of federal judges appointed Lawrence E. Walsh, a Texas Republican with a reputation as a tough prosecutor. Walsh then began a lengthy investigation of the entire matter.

*Ronald Reagan with CIA director William J. Casey.
Casey furnished North with names of arms dealers
who could buy weapons for the* contras.

THE JOINT HEARINGS. After learning about the Iran-*contra* scandal, both the Senate and the House of Representatives appointed special bipartisan committees to investigate the affair. In the spring and summer of 1987, the two committees held joint hearings. The hearings,which were carried on national television, provided viewers with the embarrassing spectacle of a presidential administration in which no one seemed to be in charge and in which American foreign policy appeared to have been handled by low-ranking executive branch officials and shady international arms merchants, and a Congress that was repeatedly deprived of information about the activities of the Reagan administration.

The highlights of the hearings were the appearances of North and Poindexter, both of whom had been granted limited immunity from prosecution, which meant they could not be charged with crimes based on their testimonies. The committee's lawyers had expected to expose North as a reckless zealot who lied and cheated to accomplish his goals. Instead, the young Marine charmed the television audience with his boyish manner and passionate, almost defiant defense of himself and the Nicaraguan *contras.*The wave of public sympathy for North caused the committee lawyers to retreat from any aggressive questioning.

Poindexter's testimony, although less dramatic than North's, was more important to the committee findings. Poindexter insisted that he had deliberately concealed the diversion of funds from the president so that Reagan could truthfully deny any knowledge of illegal acts.

In November 1987 the committees issued a joint report concluding that the arms-for-hostages deal violated the nation's stated policy regarding arms sales to Iran and dealings with terrorists. It also concluded that the diversion of funds to the Nicaraguan *contras* violated the policy of Congress as expressed in the 1984 ban on aid to the rebel group. The report avoided, however, any reference to actions by the president that might have constituted grounds for his impeachment.

GROUNDS FOR IMPEACHMENT. The president has a constitutional duty to take care that the laws be faithfully executed. By the time the joint hearings ended in August 1987, there was ample evidence that the president had failed to carry out this duty. Under a broad interpretation of the term "high crimes and misdemeanors," this was an impeachable offense.

Before the hearings had begun, however, the members of the Senate committee (which dominated the proceedings) agreed to bring up the question of Reagan's impeachment only if they had evidence that the president had knowingly diverted funds to support the Nicaraguan *contras* in violation of Congress's ban on such aid.

There were several reasons for the reluctance of the congressional leaders of both political parties to implicate the president in anything that might lead to his impeachment. The most important reason was the president himself.

President Reagan, who had been reelected in 1984 by an overwhelming margin, was personally popular. The American public, captivated by his geniality and sunny disposition, seemed willing to overlook his vagueness regarding details. (His frequent memory lapses could have resulted from the early stages of Alzheimer's disease, a condition that eventually destroys its victim's memory. Reagan revealed in November 1994 that he had the disease.)

In fact, the president's lax management style made it easy to conclude (or at least pretend) that he had been deceived by his subordinates in the face of evidence suggesting that Reagan had approved the basic policies involved in Iran-*contra* even though he may not have known all the details. Further, unlike Nixon, Reagan cooperated with the investigators—or at least gave the appearance of cooperating. (Actually, Reagan's reputation as president was damaged by the Iran-*contra* scandal whether or not he knew what was going on. If he didn't know, he was either lax or incompetent in his supervision of his subordinates in the executive branch. If he did know, he had lied in claiming that he had been deceived.)

When the scandal broke, Reagan had only a little more than two years remaining in his second term. He was prohibited from running for reelection in 1988 under the terms of the Twenty-Second Amendment. (This amendment, which was added to the Constitution in 1951, provides in part that no one shall be elected to the office of president more than twice.) Moreover, the president's age and uncertain health increased the reluctance of the congressional leaders to subject him to the stress of an impeachment investigation. Reagan, who was in his mid-seventies (he was born on February 6, 1911), had undergone cancer surgery twice during his second term.

There were other reasons as well. The congressional leaders feared that the turmoil of a presidential impeachment might encourage governments that were hostile to the United States to take actions that could threaten the country's prestige as a world power, perhaps even threaten world peace. Moreover, rebels in other countries might take advantage of the instability of American leadership to seize control of their governments. Finally, the memory of the Watergate scandal, which had taken place only twelve years before, was still fresh in people's minds. Some of the members of Congress who had taken part in the Watergate hearings still held office. Few had any desire for a repeat performance.

Despite the suspicion of many Americans that both Reagan and Bush had known about the illegal activites, Reagan served the remainder of his term. In January 1989 former Vice President Bush took the oath of office as Reagan's successor.

CONVICTIONS AND PARDONS. Meanwhile, independent counsel Lawrence Walsh and his staff continued their investigation, which resulted in the indictment of several federal officials. Both North and Poindexter were convicted of crimes stemming from the Iran-*contra* affair. (Former President Reagan testified in a videotaped interview during Poindexter's 1990 trial. Reagan, who seemed befuddled, answered, "I don't remember" to more than a hundred questions.) The convictions were later overturned on appeal because some of the evidence against these men was based on testimony for which they had been granted immunity from prosecution.

On December 24, 1992, President George Bush pardoned six other government officials who had taken part in the Iran-*contra* affair. The six had been charged with lying or otherwise participating in what Walsh called a conspiracy to cover up the scandal. Three had pleaded guilty, one had been convicted, and the other two were due to go on trial early in 1993.

Among those pardoned was Casper Weinberger, Reagan's secretary of defense during the Iran-*contra* affair. The charges against Weinberger, who had opposed the sale of arms to Iran, were based on his failure to reveal to either Congress or the Walsh investigators the existence of a personal diary that he had kept while he was secretary of defense, although he had been repeatedly questioned about the existence of such a record. Walsh criticized Bush's pardon of Weinberger and the others as the completion of a cover-up that had continued for more than six years. Walsh commented that Weinberger's withholding of his diary entries had forestalled impeachment proceedings against President Reagan.

Walsh issued a final report on his investigation of the Iran-*contra* affair in January 1994. The report was sharply critical of Congress, many Reagan administration officials, and President Bush. Walsh said that Congress's promises of immunity from prosecution in exchange for testimony prevented him from being able to convict many of those he investigated. He noted that the destruction and withholding of evidence by those under investigation hindered his efforts. He also criticized Bush's pardons as serving no public purpose. In fact, according to Walsh, the pardon of Weinberger before he went on trial prevented the prosecutors from proving the existence of a cover-up of the Iran-*contra* scandal.

In his final report Walsh said that he found evidence of the involvement of high-level Reagan administration officials in the Iran-*contra* scandal and its cover-up. Walsh named Weinberger, Secretary of State George P. Shultz, CIA Director William Casey, and the president himself as having taken part in the scandal. He also claimed that President Bush had withheld relevant notes from the investigators. Although he acknowledged that Reagan had probably acted in the belief that he was serving his country, Walsh said that if the information he uncovered had been given to the congressional investigators, the president's impeachment should have been considered.

THE IMPLICATIONS. If the evidence Walsh uncovered had been brought before the joint congressional committee in 1987, that body would have been faced with the clear political question of whether to remove a popular president from office for using his constitutional authority to obstruct the laws enacted by the people's elected representatives in Congress. Perhaps Walsh's evidence wouldn't have changed things. Perhaps the congressional leaders would have decided that allowing the president to finish his term was preferable to the upheaval of attempting to remove him from office. They might have been right about that.

Perhaps the most serious consequence of such scandals as Watergate and Iran-*contra* has been an erosion of

From left to right: former secretary of state George P. Shultz, former national security adviser John Poindexter, and former president Ronald Reagan. According to the report on Iran-contra by independent counsel Lawrence Walsh, all three were involved in the scandal and its cover-up.

the public's trust in government. We Americans have always been suspicious about our government to some extent—on guard lest it become too powerful, interfere too much in our private lives, perhaps even destroy our freedom. It was, after all, our resentment of what we regarded as a tyrannical British monarchy that started us on the road to independence in the late eighteenth century.

Yet we want to trust our government. Even though our history is riddled with political scandals, some of which have involved the highest level of government, we want to believe that our elected leaders are honest men and women whose actions are in the best interests of the American people. To believe otherwise might suggest that our experiment in self-government, now more than two hundred years old, is a failure.

Perhaps this is why American Congresses have been so reluctant to remove a president from office, even when faced with evidence of that official's abuse of the public trust—why they have seriously considered the impeachment and conviction of a president only when there was evidence of criminal acts on that official's part. Despite evidence that the framers of the Constitution did not intend that the phrase "high crimes and misdemeanors" as grounds for impeachment would apply only to crimes for which an official can be tried in a criminal court, American Congresses have continued to act as if the phrase must be applied in this way.

Andrew Johnson, who obstructed the carrying out of the laws passed by Congress in the 1860s, was not impeached until he deliberately violated a law. By focusing on this violation in the trial before the Senate, both the House members who prosecuted the case against the president and his defense lawyers avoided confronting the more serious question of whether President Johnson had abused the legitimate powers of his office in ways that were detrimental to the public interest.

Richard Nixon, in spite of a pattern of abuse of power, faced impeachment and conviction only after it became clear that by covering up his staff's involvement in the Watergate burglary he was guilty of the crime of obstruction of justice.

Ronald Reagan was not impeached despite evidence that he failed to fulfill his constitutional duty to see that the laws are faithfully carried out because the congressional leaders wanted evidence of criminal acts before they were willing to consider the issue of impeachment.

Americans differ on the question of whether a president should be removed from office for the abuse of his legitimate powers in the absence of evidence that he has also violated a law. Some argue that the turmoil resulting from a president's impeachment and trial is too high a price to pay for the removal of someone not guilty of criminal behavior. Others argue that letting a president stay in office in the face of evidence of his abuse of the public trust creates a political climate that encourages such misbehavior by future presidents. The result can be the destruction of the public's trust in both its elected officials and, ultimately, its form of government. That, in their opinion, is too high a price.

Impeachment is a difficult, time-consuming procedure, filled with political risks. An attempt to impeach a president over an honest difference of opinion on a political issue risks public condemnation of those who make such an attempt. For this reason House members have considered this drastic remedy only when there has been evidence that the president has committed a crime.

Whether House members were right or not in adopting such a narrow view of impeachment, it seems clear, at least for the present, that the best way of ridding ourselves of an unsatisfactory president is the way we have done it so often in the past—by voting that person out of office at the next election.

NOTES

CHAPTER ONE
CENSURES AND COMPLAINTS

1. Robert V. Remini, *Henry Clay: Statesman for the Union* (New York: W. W. Norton, 1991), pp. 449-451.
2. *Congressional Globe,* 27th Congress, 3d session, pp. 144-146.
3. M. N. Schnapper, ed. *Presidential Impeachment: A Documentary Overview* (Washington: Public Affairs Press, 1974), p. 13.
4. Ibid.

CHAPTER TWO
PRESIDENT ANDREW JOHNSON:
REBUILDING THE UNION

1. Hans Trefousse, *Andrew Johnson* (New York: W. W. Norton, 1989), pp. 93-94.

CHAPTER FOUR
CONGRESS INTERVENES

1. *Congressional Globe,* 39th Congress, 2d session, p. 1969.
2. Ibid., pp. 154, 319.
3. Articles of Impeachment, Article X, first specification.

Quoted in Michael Les Benedict, *The Impeachment and Trial of Andrew Johnson* (New York: W. W. Norton, 1973), p. 187.

4. James D. Richardson, ed., *A Compilation of the Messages and Papers of the Presidents, 1789-1897,* 10 vols. (Washington, 1896-1897), vol. VI, pp. 558-581; quoted in Trefousse, *Impeachment of a President* (Knoxville: University of Tennessee Press, 1975), pp. 96-97.

CHAPTER FIVE
PRESIDENT JOHNSON'S
IMPEACHMENT AND TRIAL

1. Michael Benedict's book on the Johnson impeachment, p. 172, calls the question of whether the Tenure of Office Act covered Stanton "rather unimportant." Hans L. Trefousse, *Impeachment of a President: Andrew Johnson, the Blacks, and Reconstruction* (Knoxville: University of Tennessee Press, 1975), p. 146, says: "The pretext for impeachment that Johnson provided for his impeachment was very dubious." Raoul Berger, *Impeachment: The Constitutional Problems* (Cambridge: Harvard University Press, 1973), p. 295, describes the impeachment as "an attempt to punish the President for differing with and obstructing the policy of Congress." John R. Labovitz, *Presidential Impeachment* (New Haven: Yale University Press, 1978), p. 89, describes the violation of the Tenure of Office Act as "a pretextual charge."

CHAPTER SIX
PRESIDENT RICHARD NIXON:
UNITING AMERICA

1. *Time,* November 15, 1968, p. 26.

CHAPTER SEVEN
THE REELECTION CAMPAIGN
AND WATERGATE

1. Richard Nixon, *RN: The Memoirs of Richard Nixon* (New York: Grosset & Dunlap, 1978), p. 496; quoted in Fred Em-

ery, *Watergate: The Corruption of American Politics and the Fall of Richard Nixon* (New York: Times Books, 1994), p. 32.

2. Jeb Stuart Magruder, *An American Life: One Man's Road to Watergate* (New York: Atheneum, 1974), p. 260; quoted in Emery, p. 153.

CHAPTER NINE
PRESIDENT NIXON RESIGNS

1. Schnapper, p. 14.
2. Michael Schudson, *Watergate in American Memory: How We Remember, Forget, and Reconstruct the Past* (New York: Basic Books, 1992), p. 43.
3. Nixon's remark is quoted in Stanley I. Kutler, *The Wars of Watergate: The Last Crisis of Richard Nixon* (New York: Alfred A. Knopf, 1990), p. 619; Doar's remark is quoted in John R. Labovitz, *Presidential Impeachment* (New Haven: Yale University Press, 1978), p. 120; Ford's remark is quoted in New York Times Staff, *The End of a Presidency* (New York: Holt, Rinehart & Winston, 1974), pp. 74-75.

GLOSSARY

abolitionist—a person who favored the abolition, or doing away, of slavery.

amnesty—a pardon for past offenses against a government. Amnesties are often granted for acts committed during a war to persons who were on the losing side as a means of achieving reconciliation between the former enemies.

electoral college—the group of persons chosen by the voters to elect the president and vice president of the United States. When people vote for a president and vice president, they are actually voting for presidential electors who have agreed to cast their votes for that team.

executive clemency—a reduction in a sentence or a pardon granted to an offender by a government's chief executive. The president of the United States has the authority to grant executive clemency to persons who have committed offenses against the United States.

executive privilege—the president's right to refuse to disclose confidential advice given by his staff, or other communications among members of the executive branch.

grand jury—a group of persons chosen to investigate accusations of crime. If the grand jury believes there is enough evidence against an individual to justify a trial, it indicts that person.

immunity from prosecution—freedom from being charged with a particular crime. It is often given to suspected criminals in exchange for their testimony against others involved in the same crime.

impeachment—a formal accusation, by Congress or another legislative body, of wrongdoing against a public official. The term is sometimes used incorrectly to refer to an official's removal from office. However, the official must be convicted of the charges to be removed from office.

independent counsel—a term used beginning in 1983 to replace the term "special prosecutor."

indictment—a formal accusation by a grand jury that a person has committed a crime. The indicted individual can then be brought to trial and punished if found guilty.

limited immunity—immunity from criminal prosecution based on the specific information a person gives under such a grant. Other information and evidence may be used against the person, however.

nullify—to render not legally binding. The term is often used to refer to a declaration by a governmental body that a previous action is null and void, or having no legal effect.

obstruction of justice—interfering with or otherwise hindering an official investigation of a crime by withholding pertinent information or evidence or deliberately destroying it.

override—a lawmaking body's passage of a law that has been vetoed by the chief executive. Congress can override a presidential veto by a two-thirds majority of both houses.

partisan—membership in or support of a particular group such as a political party.

political patronage—the giving of public offices or jobs to members of one's own political party without regard to an individual's qualifications.

Radical Republicans—a term used to refer to the Republican members of Congress in the period immediately after the Civil War. Actually, few of these men held radical, or extreme, views on political matters. Many were either moderates (centrists) or conservatives.

ratification—an official approval of a legal document such as a constitution. Amendments to the U.S. Constitution must be ratified by three fourths of the states before they become part of the Constitution.

recess—a short break during a session of Congress.

Reconstruction—the process of restoring the Confederate states to their former position in the Union after the Civil War.

referendum (plural: referenda)—the referral to a state's qualified voters of a political question such as a law, a new state constitution, or a constitutional amendment.

rider—a provision added to a law after action on it was supposed to have been completed.

secession—the formal act of withdrawing from an organization, such as the attempt of eleven Southern states to leave (or secede from) the Union in 1860 and 1861.

session of Congress—the period during which Congress holds regular meetings to pass laws and conduct other official business. The Constitution calls for at least one session of Congress each year.

separation of powers—the Constitution's grant of separate and distinct powers to each of the federal government's three branches (executive, legislative, and judicial).

special prosecutor—an official appointed to investigate suspected wrongdoing by federal officials, especially those who hold high offices, and to prosecute those charged with crimes as a result of such an investigation. A 1983 law changed this term to independent counsel.

states' rights—a political doctrine that holds that the role of the federal government should be limited to those items the Constitution specifically lists as federal responsibilities, leaving the states free to decide other matters for themselves.

subpoena—an official written order commanding a person to appear in court or to produce certain documents.

suffrage—the right or privilege of voting in an election of public officials.

unindicted co-conspirator—a person against whom a grand jury has enough evidence to justify an indictment but who is not actually indicted. The naming of an individual as an unindicted co-conspirator allows evidence that the grand jury has obtained concerning that person to be used in the trial of those who have been indicted.

veto—an executive's rejection of a bill passed by the legislative body.

BIBLIOGRAPHY

ANDREW JOHNSON IMPEACHMENT

Benedict, Michael Les. *The Impeachment and Trial of Andrew Johnson.* New York: W. W. Norton, 1973.

————. *A Compromise of Principle: Congressional Republicans and Reconstruction, 1863-1869.* New York: W. W. Norton, 1974.

Bowen, David Warren. *Andrew Johnson and the Negro.* Knoxville: University of Tennessee Press, 1989.

Castel, Albert. *The Presidency of Andrew Johnson.* Lawrence: The Regents Press of Kansas, 1979.

Dewitt, David Miller. *The Impeachment and Trial of Andrew Johnson. 1903.* Reprint, Madison: State Historical Society of Wisconsin, 1967.

Dunning, William Archibald. "The Impeachment and Trial of President Johnson," *Essays on the Civil War and Reconstruction. 1897.* Reprint, New York: Harper Torchbooks, 1965.

Foner, Eric. *Reconstruction: America's Unfinished Revolution, 1863-1877.* New York: Harper & Row, 1988.

————. *Short History of Reconstruction, 1863-1877*. New York: Harper & Row, 1990.

Franklin, John Hope. *Reconstruction After the Civil War.* 2d ed. Chicago: University of Chicago Press, 1994.

McKitrick, Eric L. *Andrew Johnson and Reconstruction.* Chicago: University of Chicago Press, 1960.

Thomas, Benjamin P., and Harold M. Hyman. *Stanton: The Life and Times of Lincoln's Secretary of War.* New York: Alfred A. Knopf, 1962.

Trefousse, Hans L. *Impeachment of a President: Andrew Johnson, the Blacks, and Reconstruction.* Knoxville: University of Tennessee Press, 1975.

————. *Andrew Johnson*. New York: W.W. Norton,1989.

U.S. Congress. House. *Impeachment of the President.* 40th Cong., lst sess., 1867. H. Rept. 7.

RICHARD NIXON RESIGNATION

Aitken, Jonathan. *Nixon: A Life*. Washington: Regnery Publishing, 1993.

Bernstein, Carl, and Bob Woodward. *All the President's Men.* New York: Simon & Schuster, 1974.

Colodny, Len, and Robert Gettlin. *Silent Coup: The Removal of a President.* New York: St. Martin's Paperbacks, 1992.

Emery, Fred. *Watergate: The Corruption of American Politics and the Fall of Richard Nixon.* New York: Times Books, 1994.

Facts on File. 1973-1975.

Gitlin, Todd. *The Sixties: Years of Hope, Days of Rage.* New York: Bantam Books, 1993.

Hougan, Jim. *Secret Agenda: Watergate, Deep Throat and the CIA.* New York: Random House, 1984.

Kutler, Stanley I. *The Wars of Watergate: The Last Crisis of Richard Nixon.* New York: Alfred A. Knopf, 1990.

LaRue, L. H. *Political Discourse: A Case Study of the Watergate Affair.* Athens: University of Georgia Press, 1988.

Lukas, J. Anthony. *Nightmare: The Underside of the Nixon Years.* New York: The Viking Press, 1976.

New York Times Staff. *The End of a Presidency.* New York: Holt, Rinehart & Winston, 1974.

Schudson, Michael. *Watergate in American Memory: How We Remember, Forget, and Reconstruct the Past.* New York: Basic Books, 1992.

Time. 1968-1972.

U.S. Congress. House. *Impeachment of Richard M. Nixon, President of the United States.* 93d Cong., 2d sess., 1974. H. Rept. 93-1305.

U.S. Congress. Senate. *The Final Report of the Select Committee on Presidential Campaign Activities.* 93d Cong., 2d sess., 1974. S. Rept. 93-981.

White, Theodore H. *The Making of the President 1972.* New York: Atheneum Publishers, 1973.

Woodward, Bob, and Carl Bernstein. *The Final Days.* New York: Simon & Schuster, 1976.

IRAN-*CONTRA* SCANDAL

Crabb, Cecil V., Jr., and Pat M. Holt. *Invitation to Struggle: Congress, the President, and Foreign Policy,* 3d ed. Washington: Congressional Quarterly Press, 1989.

Draper, Theodore. *A Very Thin Line: The Iran-Contra Affairs.* New York: Hill & Wang, 1991.

Facts on File. 1992-1994.

Hersh, Seymour M. "The Iran-Contra Committees: Did They Protect Reagan?" *New York Times Magazine,* April 29, 1990, pp. 46-78.

Mayer, Jane, and Doyle McManus. *Landslide: The Unmaking of the President 1984-1988.* Boston: Houghton Mifflin Co., 1988.

*Time.*1986-1988.

GENERAL REFERENCE

Berger, Raoul. *Impeachment: The Constitutional Problems.* Cambridge: Harvard University Press, 1973.

Brant, Irving. *Impeachment: Trials and Errors.* New York: Alfred A. Knopf, 1972.

Congressional Globe, 23d Cong., lst sess.; 27th Cong., 2d and 3d sess.

Ehrlich, Walter. *Presidential Impeachment: An American Dilemma.* St. Charles, MO: Forum Press, 1974.

Labovitz, John R. *Presidential Impeachment.* New Haven: Yale University Press, 1978.

Remini, Robert V. *Henry Clay: Statesman for the Union.* New York: W. W. Norton, 1991.

Schnapper, M. N., ed. *Presidential Impeachment: A Documentary Overview.* Washington: Public Affairs Press, 1974.

INDEX

Page numbers in *italics* refer to illustrations.

Ervin, Sam, 95, 98, *99*
Ervin Watergate Committee,
  95, 98-100, *99*, 108, 112,
  114
Ethics in Government Act of
  1978, 121, 129
Executive clemency, 90, 98,
  99
Executive privilege, 100,
  111, 114
Ex Parte Milligan, 36

Farwell, Leonard, 21
Federal Bureau of Investiga-
  tion (FBI), 69, 70, 88-90,
  97, 116, 120-121
Federalist, The (Hamilton,
  Madison, and Jay), 19
Federal judges, 18, 20
Fessenden, William Pitt, 59,
  60
Fielding, Lewis, 74, 84,
  85
First Bank of the United
  States, 12
Ford, Gerald, 108, 117-119
Foreign Assistance Act,
  Hughes-Ryan Amend-
  ment to (1974), 120
Foreign Intelligence Surveil-
  lance Act of 1978, 120
Fortieth Congress, 41, 45-
  47, 49-50
Fowler, Joseph S., 59
Freedmen's Bureau, 23, 33,
  34, 36, 50

Gonzalez, Virgilio R., 85
Grant, Ulysses S., 22, 44,
  47, 54, 56
Gray, L. Patrick, *88*, 88, 89,
  95-96
Grimes, James W., 59, 61
Gulf of Tonkin resolution,
  66

Haig, Alexander, 100, 109,
  110
Haldeman, H.R., *71*, 71-72,
  78, 82, 87, 89, 96, 98, 99,
  106, 108, 109, 116, 119
Hamilton, Andrew, 19
Hamlin, Hannibal, 26
Harlan, James, 40
Harrison, William Henry, 16
Henderson, John B., 59
High crimes and misde-
  meanors, 18-19, 45, 49,
  62, 132, 137
Ho Chi Minh, 66
Hoover, J. Edgar, 70, 72, 73,
  88
Humphrey, Hubert H., 65,
  67
Hunt, E. Howard, 72, 73-74,
  85-88, 90, 94, 96, 97, 99,
  109, 119
Huston, Tom, 70, 72, 80

Intelligence Oversight Act of
  1980, 120
Internal Revenue Service
  (IRS), 81, 116

St. Clair, James, 109, 111,
114, 115
Saturday Night Massacre,
103-104
Schlesinger, James, 115
Schofield, John M., 51, 61
Scowcroft, Brent, 127
Second Bank of the United
States, 11, 12
Separation of powers doc-
trine, 15-16
Sessions of Congress, 27
Seward, William H., 34
Seymour, Horatio, 61
Sheridan, Philip S., 46, 47
Sherman, William T., 34
Shultz, George P., 135, *136*
Sickles, Daniel E., 48
Sirica, John J., 93-95, *94*,
102, 105, 106, 108, 109,
111, 114, 116
Slavery, 22, 25, 28, 32
Sloan, Hugh W., Jr., 72, 79,
98
Somoza, Anastasio, 124
Speed, James, 40
Stanbery, Henry, 46
Stans, Maurice, 79, 80, 98
Stanton, Edwin M., 41, *47*,
53-54, 57-59, 61
State constitutions, 28, 30,
51-52
States' rights, 36, 40
Stennis, John, 102
Stephens, Alexander H., 31

Stevens, Thaddeus, 37, *55*,
56, 62
Strachan, Gordon C., 71, 82,
109, 119
Sturgis, Frank A., 85
Suffrage, 29, 30, 43-44, 48,
51
Sumner, Charles, 37
Supreme Court of the United
States, 38, 57, 59, 70, 73,
111, 114-115, 120

Taney, Roger B., 11, 13
Tenure of Office Act of 1867,
44-45, 52-54, 56-59, 61
Thirty-Eighth Congress, 26
Thirty-Ninth Congress, 26,
31, 42-45, 49, 50, 56
Thomas, George H., 47
Thomas, Lorenzo, 54
Tower, John, 127
Treason, 18, 19
Trumbull, Lyman, 59
Twenty-Third Congress, 9
Tyler, John, 16, *17*, 18, 20

Unindicted co-conspirator,
109, 114

Van Winkle, Peter G., 59
Vietnam War, 64, 66, 69, 70,
93, 116, 119
Voting rights, 29, 30, 43-44,
48, 51